THE
FIRE ISLAND
COOKBOOK

THE
FIRE ISLAND
COOKBOOK

Mike DeSimone

and

Jeff Jenssen

EMILY BESTLER BOOKS
—
ATRIA
New York   London   Toronto   Sydney   New Delhi

ATRIA BOOKS

A Division of Simon & Schuster, Inc.
1230 Avenue of the Americas
New York, NY 10020

EMILY
BESTLER
BOOKS

First Emily Bestler Books/Atria Books hardcover edition April 2012

EMILY BESTLER BOOKS / ATRIA BOOKS and colophons are
trademarks of Simon & Schuster, Inc.

For information about special discounts for bulk purchases,
please contact Simon & Schuster Special Sales at
1-866-506-1949 or business@simonandschuster.com.

The Simon & Schuster Speakers Bureau can bring authors
to your live event. For more information or to book an event,
contact the Simon & Schuster Speakers Bureau at
1-866-248-3049 or visit our website at www.simonspeakers.com.

Designed by Jason Snyder

Food photography by Frances Janisch

Manufactured in the United States of America

10   9   8   7   6   5   4   3   2   1

Library of Congress Cataloging-in-Publication Data

DeSimone, Mike.
The Fire Island cookbook / by Mike DeSimone and Jeff Jenssen.
    p.   cm.
1. Cooking, American. 2. Dinners and dining. 3. Cookbooks. I. Jenssen, Jeff. II. Title.
TX715.D467   2012
641.5973—dc23   2011044438

ISBN 978-1-4516-3293-4
ISBN 978-1-4516-3294-1 (ebook)

To our family and friends, who have always
welcomed us with generosity of spirit, glass, and table

CONTENTS

FOREWORD

by Al Roker

I love sitting down with a good cookbook.

The best allow you to imagine yourself in a world-class kitchen, actually possessing the ability to make what's on the page.

Sadly, those cookbooks are few and far between. I find myself getting confused just reading the darn recipe. Odds are, I don't have any of the ingredients and none of the equipment, and I lack the advanced skills the recipe calls for. Hey, cookbook writers, I don't plan on spending half the day in a kitchen equipment store looking for a truffle zester or whatever arcane piece of kitchen gadgetry you call for.

And the commentary that goes along with the recipes can be stuffy, pompous, and downright boring. Sorry, I don't have a degree in gastro-nuclear-physics. I don't understand what you're saying! English, please.

Then there's *The Fire Island Cookbook*. Not only can you imagine making these recipes, you can hear Mike and Jeff telling you great stories while you're cooking. I know these guys. I know their voices. Just imagine them in your kitchen helping you cook *and* picking out great wines to go with your meal!

The casual, laid-back atmosphere of Fire Island is captured perfectly within the pages of this book. So relax and try the menus in Mike and Jeff's baby, *The Fire Island Cookbook*. No matter what the season, there is always a perfect reason to turn to this cookbook again and again.

Enjoy!!!

THE
FIRE ISLAND
COOKBOOK

INTRODUCTION

Summer is the time of year that we love the best, and all we can think about the whole season is heading to the beach. Sometimes it's just for the weekend, and at other times we are away for weeks at a stretch, but among the joys of a beach house are having a kitchen and also having time to prepare dinner for or with family and friends. In our travels as wine and food writers, we have had the wonderful opportunity to eat dinner in restaurants around the globe—and the first thing we want to do when we get home is try out new dishes on the people we love. Since everyone slows down a little when the heat sets in, summer seems like the best time for everyone to get together and enjoy a dinner using fresh seasonal ingredients.

Summer is also the height of the mouthwatering produce season—from asparagus to zucchini, served hot or cold, raw or cooked, simply grilled or smothered in sauce. No matter if you are serving fish straight from the sea or prime cuts of aged meat, everything tastes better when it is presented with style. A well-laid table and an attractively arranged plate turn a meal into a feast for all of the senses, and a few extra moments in the kitchen will keep your friends talking about your cooking for the rest of the summer. And let's be honest: as much as we all love to play host, the best kind of houseguests are those who show up with their favorite cookbooks, a bag of groceries, and a few bottles of wine, allowing *you* to be the guest in your own home.

Fire Island—a barrier island less than fifty miles from New York City—is home to one of the many beaches we spend time at. On Fire Island, dining-out options are slim, so most people eat dinner in. We took Fire Island and the idea of cooking at your home-away-from-home as our starting point, but we have shared houses with friends (here in the States and all around the world) that have run the gamut in terms of size and style of accommodation: beach cottages on Fire Island, oceanfront mansions in the Hamptons, farmhouses in Tuscany, villas in Spain, bungalows on Cape Cod, and grand Victorians on the Great Lakes. What they all have in common is the break from our ordinary routine. Days spent lolling in the waves or lounging under an umbrella leave plenty of time to decide what to have for dinner.

Many of the menus in this cookbook involve dishes that can be prepared ahead of time and finished at the last minute, so you can do your prep work in the morning and then spend your day by the water along with the rest of the gang. They can also be divided up among the group, with one or two people tackling each course, so that nobody has to work too hard to get dinner on the table. With fourteen menus to choose from, there is one for each weekend from Memorial Day to Labor Day, or one per night for a two-week stay at the beach.

Most of the meals presented here are meant to be served one plate at a time, with the exception of Peak Summer Produce, Fourth of July Pool Party, and Labor Day Caribbean Barbecue, which are set up family-style. Almost all also involve both grilled food and cold dishes, except for Rainy Day French Menu and Height of the Empire; these two are optimal if you get hit with a little stormy weather and the best plan is staying indoors to cook. Other dinners, such as Noche Caliente Spanish Dinner, Portside in Puerto Vallarta, and Villa in Tuscany play on our travels: we have brought home our best finds to create recipes that everyone will enjoy. We have also recommended wine to pair with each dish, and have given two choices with each main course. If you can't find the exact one that we mention, ask for something from the same region, made from the same grape. Some menus include an *apéritif* or *aperitivo*; everyone enjoys a before-dinner libation, and even if dinner is not quite ready as the crowd begins to gather in the kitchen, you still feel like a good host as you offer your friends a cold drink.

Whether a house on the beach is your dream vacation, an occasional weekend destination, or the place you call home from April to October, you are sure to enjoy this collection of recipes, menus, photos, and entertaining ideas. Wherever you are in the world right now, take a moment, close your eyes, slide onto a bench on the upper deck of a ferry, let the mainland slip away, feel the cool spray against your skin, taste the salt in the air, and prepare yourself to enjoy one of the best dinners you, your family, and your friends have ever shared.

1

NOCHE CALIENTE
SPANISH DINNER

This menu brings together the briny taste of the sea with the juicy pleasure of a well-aged steak. Perfectly spiced gazpacho, crafted from ripe tomatoes and locally grown peppers, stimulates the appetite in anticipation of courses to follow. We came back from Spain with the inspiration for this dinner, but the combination of flavors and textures is right at home anywhere there's a cooling body of water and a stretch of shore.

Summertime dinners in Spain start around 10 p.m., when the sun finally sets and the air grows deliciously cool—even cool enough for you to enjoy a glass of red wine pulled from your own cellar. We often dine on the terrace of our house in Spain until well past three in the morning, and we always make sure there's plenty of extra wine on hand in case we're keeping the neighbors awake. Conversation flows back and forth in English and Spanish, and although verb tenses are always a challenge, our friends tell us that when it comes to our cooking, nothing is lost in translation.

GAZPACHO
WINE: *Burgáns Albariño*

GAMBAS PIL PIL
WINE: *Vivanco Rosé*

SPANISH RUBBED STEAK
WINE: *Marqués de Riscal Reserva or Roda Reserva*

HELADO MALAGUEÑO
(RUM RAISIN ICE CREAM)
WINE: *Jorge Ordoñez, Victoria Number 2*

GAZPACHO

MAKES 8 SERVINGS

A cold soup that can be prepared ahead of time is an ideal start to dinner on Fire Island—or whichever beach you call home.

½ loaf of yesterday's French bread

4 cloves garlic

¾ cup extra virgin olive oil

8 pounds local tomatoes (8 to 12 tomatoes), seeded and cut into large chunks

1 green bell pepper, cut into large pieces

1 Italian frying pepper, cut into large pieces

1 jalapeño pepper, seeded and cut into large pieces

1 cucumber, peeled and cut into large chunks

1 medium Spanish onion, cut into large chunks

1 tablespoon salt

1 teaspoon ground cumin

¼ cup sherry vinegar

Chopped tomatoes, green bell pepper, and onion, for garnish

1. Using your hands, break the bread into big chunks and soak in water for 10 minutes.

2. Squeeze the excess water out of the bread and transfer the bread to a food processor. Add the garlic and oil and process until smooth. Add the tomatoes, peppers, cucumber, onion, salt, and cumin. Process until you achieve a smooth consistency. Add the vinegar and process for 30 seconds. Blend in 1½ to 2¼ cups cold water, depending on the desired consistency, and refrigerate until ready to serve.

3. To serve, divide the gazpacho among 8 bowls and garnish with chopped tomatoes, green pepper, and onion.

WINE
Burgáns Albariño

ALBARIÑO; RIAS BAIXAS, GALICIA, SPAIN

The rich minerality and bright apple notes of this wine from Galicia pair beautifully with this fresh and spicy gazpacho.

GAMBAS PIL PIL

MAKES 8 SERVINGS

Sizzling, spicy shrimp are a favorite at the *merenderos* (open-air bars) that line the beaches on the Costa del Sol. The shrimp are great served as an appetizer, with a rosado, a light, fruit-scented rosé wine.

1⅓ cups olive oil

8 tablespoons (1 stick) butter, melted

1 teaspoon Tabasco or hot sauce

6 tablespoons hot paprika

4 teaspoons coarse sea salt

1 teaspoon cayenne pepper

12 cloves garlic, slivered

32 jumbo shrimp (see Note), peeled and deveined

Crusty Italian or French bread, for dunking in sauce

WINE: *Vivanco Rosé*

GARNACHA AND TEMPRANILLO; RIOJA, SPAIN

This light and fruity rosé made from Spanish varietals has the crispness of a white wine and the mouthfeel of a red.

1. Preheat the broiler.

2. Combine the oil, butter, Tabasco, paprika, salt, cayenne, and garlic in a 2-cup glass measuring cup. Place 4 shrimp in each of 8 small ovenproof ramekins or dishes. Divide the spicy garlic oil among the ramekins.

3. Arrange the ramekins on a baking sheet and broil until the shrimp are red-pink and the oil is sizzling, 3 to 4 minutes.

4. To serve, place each ramekin on a slightly larger dish and be sure to yell "Hot plate!!!" as you slide it onto the table. Serve with bread to soak up all that good garlicky-hot oil.

NOTE: You can substitute 48 or 56 slightly smaller shrimp for the 32 jumbo shrimp.

SPANISH RUBBED STEAK

MAKES 8 SERVINGS

This brings the flavors of Spain home to the beach—paprika and cayenne spice up your steak on a hot summer night.

1 cup olive oil

¼ cup kosher salt

¼ cup sweet paprika

4 teaspoons sugar

1 teaspoon cayenne pepper

1 teaspoon dried oregano

8 filet mignon steaks (5 to 6 ounces each; see Tip)

1. Combine the oil, salt, paprika, sugar, cayenne, and oregano in a small bowl or glass measuring cup. Spoon a small amount of the paste onto the top of each steak, spread, turn over, and repeat on the other side. Marinate for at least 4 hours and up to 24 in the refrigerator. If marinating for longer than a few hours, cover with plastic wrap or place in a plastic bag.

2. Preheat the broiler or a grill. Broil or grill for about 4 minutes per side for medium-rare.

TIP: For uniform, round filets, shape the steaks and tie each with a piece of kitchen twine before rubbing. And remember to have sharp scissors handy to remove the twine before serving.

WINE:

Marqués de Riscal Reserva

TEMPRANILLO, GRACIANO, AND MAZUELO; RIOJA, SPAIN

This traditional Riojan blend stands up to the strong spice of grilled meat.

OR

Roda Reserva

TEMPRANILLO AND GRACIANO; RIOJA, SPAIN

More modern in style, this full-bodied red has notes of ripe red cherries and aromatic herbs.

HELADO MALAGUEÑO
(RUM RAISIN ICE CREAM)

MAKES 8 SERVINGS

Helado malagueño is a favorite on the beaches of Spain—and it could become your summertime favorite as well!

1 cup packed raisins

⅔ cup dark rum

12 large egg yolks

1 cup sugar

2 cups whole milk

2 cups heavy cream

WINE:
*Jorge Ordoñez,
Victoria Number 2*

MUSCAT; SIERRAS DE MALAGA, SPAIN

Made from partially dried grapes, this honey-flavored dessert wine is a match made in heaven for rum raisin ice cream.

1. Combine the raisins and rum in a 2-cup glass measuring cup. Cover and let stand for 2 hours. Pour off the rum, reserving 6 tablespoons. Add the 6 tablespoons back to the raisins.

2. Whisk the egg yolks and sugar together in a glass bowl until creamy.

3. Bring the milk and cream to a boil in a heavy-bottomed saucepan. Stirring constantly, use a ½-cup measure or large spoon to gradually add the hot milk mixture to the eggs and sugar. Return the mixture to the saucepan. Stir over medium heat until the custard is thick enough to coat the back of a spoon, 10 to 15 minutes. Do not let boil.

4. Pour the custard into a glass bowl. Stir in the raisins and rum. Refrigerate until cold.

5. Pour the custard into an ice cream maker and freeze according to the manufacturer's instructions.

6. Transfer to a covered plastic container and place in the freezer until ready to serve.

2
RAINY DAY FRENCH MENU

Into each life a little rain must fall . . . literally and figuratively. A few years back while bicycling through the Burgundy region in France, Jeff got five flats in one day. As luck would have it, we ran out of spares and patch kits in the town of Puligny-Montrachet, which happens to be the home of some of our favorite wines. "Stuck" in the town tasting room while waiting for a taxi large enough to accommodate us, our bikes, and the cases of wine we were buying, we tried a multitude of fabulous wines and became friends with some of the local vintners. When we finally made our way back to town, the fellow who rented us the bicycles apologized by making a reservation at a wonderful restaurant, and he also had a lovely bottle sent over to our table. Possibly the best bit of luck all day was experiencing this wonderful beef bourguignon, made with fork-tender short ribs.

APERITIF: *Henriot Champagne Blanc de Blancs*

CHICKEN LIVER PÂTÉ
WINE: *Brotte La Doucejoie*

PROVENÇAL BLACK OLIVE AND ONION TART
WINE: *Château d'Aqueria Rosé*

ELEGANT BEEF BOURGUIGNON
WINE: *Louis Jadot Pommard or Bouchard Père et Fils Aloxe-Corton*

STIFF MASHED POTATOES CROSS-CUT POTATOES

MESCLUN SALAD WITH ROQUEFORT-DIJON VINAIGRETTE

BAKED CRÈME BRÛLÉE
DIGESTIF: *Bénédictine Liqueur*

When it rains at the beach, there is often little more to do than read, watch movies, or cook. The dishes in this meal are a little bit heavier and take longer to cook than many of the others you will find here. So the next time a little rain falls into your life, brighten up everyone's day by filling the house with the wonderful scents of a well-prepared French dinner.

CHICKEN LIVER PÂTÉ

MAKES 8 SERVINGS

We have never really understood the question "So what am I, chopped liver?" Quite frankly, if you are this particular French version of chopped liver, you will be adored by everyone, and there won't be enough of you to go around.

½ cup all-purpose flour

1 teaspoon salt

½ teaspoon ground black pepper

1½ pounds chicken livers

½ pound (2 sticks) butter, at room temperature, plus extra for the ramekins

3 shallots, sliced

¼ cup brandy

2 tablespoons butcher-cut black pepper

2 French baguettes, sliced, for serving

Dijon mustard, for garnish

WINE:
Brotte La Doucejoie

MUSCAT; BEAUMES DE VENISE, RHÔNE VALLEY, FRANCE

The buttery richness of pâté is perfectly complemented by the bright acidity of this sweet wine.

1. Combine the flour, salt, and ground pepper in a gallon-size resealable plastic bag. Rinse and drain the chicken livers.

2. Heat 4 tablespoons (½ stick) of the butter in a large skillet. Add the shallots and cook until softened. Add the chicken livers to the bag of flour and shake until coated. Add the livers to the pan and cook until browned on all sides.

3. Transfer the livers to a food processor. Add the brandy to the skillet and stir to get up any browned bits. Add the pan juices and butcher-cut pepper to the food processer and process until well blended but coarsely ground. Let the mixture cool for 15 minutes, then add the remaining butter 2 tablespoons at a time and process until the mixture is a smooth paste.

4. Grease eight 5-ounce ramekins (see Note) with the extra softened butter and spoon the pâté mixture into each. Refrigerate for about 4 hours before serving. (May be made the day before.)

5. To serve, place 1 ramekin in the center of each plate and surround with sliced French bread. Garnish the plate with Dijon mustard.

NOTE: You may use 3 miniature loaf pans if you prefer sliced pâté.

PROVENÇAL BLACK OLIVE AND ONION TART

MAKES 8 SERVINGS

This simple tart uses pungent niçoise olives that are grown in Provence. It combines the earthy flavors of root vegetables with the salty, sun-drenched olives. While this is baking, your rainy-day house will be filled with the buttery pastry aromas of southern France. When we cook this on Fire Island, it never fails to bring the neighbors around sniffing for a taste.

Dough

1¼ cups all-purpose flour

1 teaspoon salt

¼ teaspoon finely ground rosemary

8 tablespoons (1 stick) butter, cut into bits

1 egg

2 to 3 teaspoons ice water

Filling

2 tablespoons olive oil

2 tablespoons butter

3 small Vidalia onions, coarsely diced

¾ cup pitted niçoise olives

½ teaspoon ground black pepper

¼ teaspoon salt

Garnish

Eight 4-inch rosemary sprigs

1. To make the dough: Combine the flour, salt, and rosemary in a bowl. Using your fingers, rub in the butter until the mixture looks like small bread crumbs. Make a well in the center and add the egg. Mix well with your hands and add ice water as necessary until the dough holds together. Remove the dough from the bowl and work into a ball. Be careful not to overwork the dough, as it can get "tough." Wrap the dough in plastic wrap and refrigerate for 1 hour.

2. Remove the dough from the refrigerator and roll out to a 12-inch circle on a lightly floured surface. Fit the dough into a buttered 11-inch tart pan with a removable bottom. Place the pan in the refrigerator for 30 minutes.

3. To make the filling: Heat the oil in a skillet, then add the butter. Add the onions and cook until soft and light golden-brown. Add the olives, pepper, and salt and continue to cook for 10 minutes. Set the filling aside.

(continued)

WINE:

Château d'Aqueria Rosé

GRENACHE BLEND; TAVEL,
RHÔNE, FRANCE

This zingy yet fruity wine
from Provence will not be
overpowered by the olives and
onions in this Provençal favorite.

4. Preheat the oven to 400°F. Remove the chilled tart pan from the refrigerator, prick the bottom with a fork, and bake for 10 minutes. Remove from the oven and spread the filling evenly in the tart shell. Return to the oven and bake until the crust is golden in color, 18 to 22 minutes. Remove and place on a rack to cool.

5. To serve, cut the tart into 8 wedges. Garnish each wedge with a rosemary sprig.

ELEGANT BEEF BOURGUIGNON

MAKES 8 SERVINGS

Our favorite beef bourguignon is made from fork-tender short ribs. Each plate is a work of art, with its own basket of cross-cut French fries. This easy but elegant preparation is sure to delight your most discriminating houseguests. They'll be talking about you and your main course for weeks to come.

About ⅓ cup olive oil

2 onions, chopped

2 large carrots, chopped

1 medium parsnip, peeled and chopped

Salt and ground black pepper

8 short ribs of beef (about 4 pounds)

½ cup all-purpose flour

Red Burgundy wine to cover the beef (at least 1 bottle)

2 teaspoons Dijon mustard

2 pinches herbes de Provence

Stiff Mashed Potatoes (recipe follows)

Cross-Cut Potatoes (recipe follows)

1. Heat ⅓ cup oil in a large heavy-bottomed pot or Dutch oven over medium heat. Add the onions, carrots, and parsnip and cook, stirring, until soft and golden, about 5 minutes. Season with salt and pepper to taste.

2. Toss the short ribs with the flour in a 1-gallon resealable plastic bag until coated. Move the vegetables to the side of the pot, adding a little more oil to the center of the pot if necessary, and add 4 short ribs. Cook until browned on one side, 3 to 4 minutes. Turn and cook until browned on the second side, 3 to 4 minutes. Transfer to a plate. Repeat with the other 4 short ribs.

3. When the second batch of ribs is browned, add the first 4 ribs back to the pot. Add enough red wine to cover. Stir in the mustard, the herbes de Provence, and a little more salt and pepper. Bring to a boil, then reduce to a simmer, cover, and cook until the meat is falling off the bone, about 2½ hours.

4. Meanwhile, prepare the mashed potatoes and cross-cut fries.

(continued)

5. Remove the ribs from the pot and set aside. Return the pot to medium heat and boil, uncovered, to reduce the liquid by one-third. When the meat is cool enough to handle, shred with a fork and discard the bones. Reduce the heat under the pot, return the meat to the pot, and simmer for about 30 minutes.

6. To assemble the dish, place a 3½-inch round biscuit cutter in the center of a plate and use a soup spoon to fill halfway with mashed potatoes. Using a slotted spoon, add some beef bourguignon to the top half of the ring, draining well as you remove each spoonful from the pot. Carefully remove the biscuit cutter. When all the mounds have been plated, place 5 or 6 cross-cut potato slices around the outside of each serving, forming a "basket." Serve immediately.

STIFF MASHED POTATOES

MAKES 8 SERVINGS

Mashed potatoes are the ultimate comfort food, especially when combined with tender braised beef.

3 pounds small to medium red
    potatoes, quartered

⅔ cup milk

4 tablespoons butter

Salt and ground black pepper

1. Place the potatoes in a pot of salted cold water and bring to a boil. Reduce the heat to medium and cook until fork-tender, 15 to 20 minutes.

2. Meanwhile, microwave the milk and butter in a glass measuring cup in 15-second increments until the butter is melted, 30 to 45 seconds.

3. Drain the potatoes and return to the pot. Add about half of the milk mixture and salt and pepper to taste. Mash with a hand masher. Add more milk mixture as needed. For this recipe, the stiffer the potatoes, the better, because you need them to hold their shape.

CROSS-CUT POTATOES

MAKES 8 SERVINGS

Better than the best French fries from your favorite steak house, these cross-cut potato wedges form the "basket" that frames your delicious beef bourguignon. This recipe requires a mandoline.

4 large white potatoes

1 quart vegetable oil, for frying

Fine sea salt

1. Peel the potatoes and slice them on a mandoline set for ridge or cross-cut.

2. Heat the oil to 375°F in a large high-sided pan. Fry the potato slices, a few at a time, until golden brown. Drain on paper towels and dust with sea salt.

MESCLUN SALAD WITH ROQUEFORT-DIJON VINAIGRETTE

MAKES 8 SERVINGS

Anytime we eat a dish involving Roquefort, a strong French blue cheese, we laugh about the time we visited a Michelin-starred restaurant in the south of France. When the glass-covered cheese cart was rolled to our table and the *fromagier* pointed to each specimen and pronounced its name, our friend Greg asked if there was any Roquefort that evening. In high-attitude Franglish, Monsieur Fromagier, as he has come to be known in our retelling, stood straight up, inhaled swiftly and loudly through both nostrils, and declared, "Monsieur, for Roquefort, one can go to the *supermarché.*" Only in France, kids, only in France!

½ cup extra virgin olive oil

3 tablespoons balsamic vinegar

3 ounces Roquefort cheese, crumbled

2 teaspoons Dijon mustard

8 ounces mesclun

Fleur de sel

WINE:

You can continue drinking your main-course Burgundy wine with this salad.

1. Combine the oil, vinegar, cheese, and mustard in a glass measuring cup. Allow to sit at room temperature until the cheese is softened.

2. Divide the mesclun among 8 salad plates. Briskly stir the dressing with a fork or small whisk until the cheese and mustard are incorporated. Drizzle a small amount of dressing over each serving. Sprinkle a few grains of fleur de sel onto each and serve.

BAKED CRÈME BRÛLÉE

MAKES 8 SERVINGS

Crème brûlée barely needs an introduction. Mike sends his back if he can't "crack" the surface with his spoon.

12 egg yolks

½ cup plus ¼ cup sugar

2 cups heavy cream

1½ teaspoons vanilla extract

DIGESTIF:
Bénédictine Liqueur

FÉCAMP, NORMANDY, FRANCE

Created by Benedictine monks, this lightly herbal and citrusy liqueur feels like honey in your mouth.

1. Preheat the oven to 300°F. Whisk the egg yolks and ½ cup of the sugar together in a large bowl until the sugar is dissolved and the mixture is pale yellow. Whisk in the cream and vanilla, whisking until blended. Strain into another large bowl.

2. Slowly pour the mixture into eight 5-ounce ramekins, being sure to skim off any bubbles. Place the ramekins in a roasting pan filled with 1 to 1¼ inches of water. Bake until set at the edges but still loose in the middle, about 45 minutes. Remove from the oven and let cool in the water bath. Remove the ramekins from the water bath and chill for at least 2 hours. (May be made up to this point 2 days in advance.)

3. At serving time, sprinkle about 1½ teaspoons of sugar over each ramekin of crème brûlée. Use a small handheld torch to melt the sugar. (You can buy a torch at kitchen equipment stores just for this purpose.) If there is no torch in the house, borrow one from the folks next door, or just place the ramekins under the broiler until the sugar is melted.

TIP: *Crème brûlée* is French for "burnt cream," but the sugar should crack like glass and still taste sweet. When melting the sugar on crème brûlée, you have to caramelize it to the point that it can be cracked with the tip or back of a teaspoon. If you want to practice before trying this out in front of dinner guests, test your technique on a ramekin of store-bought pudding or yogurt while nobody else is around.

3

PEAK SUMMER PRODUCE

Picture yourself at a farmers' market in the country at the height of vegetable season. Breathe in the strong fragrance of ripe, red tomatoes and leafy green basil. Celebrating the flavors of summer, this meal combines staples of Italian-American cooking in surprising ways, with delightful results. *Crudo*—fresh raw tomato sauce—served over hot pasta is a favorite in our home, and Basil Vanilla Ice Cream is another unexpected pleasure.

Except for dessert, these dishes are best served family-style, so make sure your bowls and platters are ready to be put to use.

The ice cream is probably best made a night—or even a week—before. The beauty of the *crudo* is that it "cooks" on the counter all day, the flavors mingling to perfection, with the heady scent of tomatoes and basil brought to their climax when tossed with just-boiled fusilli. The dressing for the asparagus can also be made in the

APERITIVO: *Martini Rosato on the Rocks*

GRILLED ASPARAGUS IN PANCETTA-SHALLOT VINAIGRETTE
WINE: *Bigi Orvieto Classico*

FUSILLI WITH "CRUDO" TOMATO SAUCE
WINE: *Planeta Rosé*

PESTO-SMOTHERED GRILLED CHICKEN BREAST
WINE: *Carpineto Dogajolo Bianco or St. Michael Eppan*

SALAD OF WILTED SPINACH, OIL-CURED BLACK OLIVES, AND BLOOD ORANGES
WINE: *San Angelo Pinot Grigio*

BASIL VANILLA ICE CREAM
WINE: *Villa Rosa Moscato d'Asti*

APERITIVO:

Martini Rosato
on the Rocks

This delicate vermouth from the north of Italy primes your palate with a fresh fruity attack and lingers with flavors of clove and cinnamon.

morning, and if you start the water for the pasta and turn on the grill the second you walk in the door, you can have dinner on the table the moment your guests arrive. But why not take a few minutes to enjoy a Martini Rosato with your summer family first, to get everyone in the mood for a feast that will take you from the beach to Tuscany in no time flat.

GRILLED ASPARAGUS IN PANCETTA-SHALLOT VINAIGRETTE

MAKES 8 SERVINGS

Hiking in the hills above our Spanish house we find wild spring asparagus. We love the old men who collect handfuls and then sell them at the market for one euro per bundle. Our friends on Fire Island love this simple preparation.

6 tablespoons olive oil

3 tablespoons kosher salt

64 spears asparagus (about 3 pounds)

4 thin slices pancetta

6 tablespoons extra virgin olive oil

2 tablespoons balsamic vinegar

2 small shallots, finely diced

Maldon salt or fleur de sel

Coarsely ground black pepper

WINE:
Bigi Orvieto Classico

TREBBIANO GRECHETTO BLEND; ORVIETO, UMBRIA, ITALY

This lovely wine from the town of Orvieto in Umbria has aromas of fresh peaches and almonds.

1. Preheat the grill.

2. Place 2 tablespoons olive oil and 1 tablespoon salt in a resealable plastic bag. Add one-third of the asparagus and shake to coat evenly. Repeat 2 more times. Grill the asparagus for 2 to 3 minutes until they begin to brown. Transfer to a large serving platter and set aside uncovered.

3. Cook the pancetta in a large cast-iron skillet until almost crisp, turning once. Drain on paper towels, but reserve the drippings. When cool, dice or finely crumble.

4. Combine the extra virgin olive oil, pan drippings, vinegar, shallots, and pancetta in a glass measuring cup. Stir well and cover with plastic wrap until serving time.

5. When ready to serve, drizzle the vinaigrette evenly over the grilled asparagus. Top with a few small pinches of Maldon salt or fleur de sel and a few twists of black pepper.

FUSILLI WITH "CRUDO" TOMATO SAUCE

MAKES 8 SERVINGS

When Mike was growing up in New Jersey, his mother would buy copy-paper boxes filled with slightly bruised tomatoes for just a few dollars. The really banged-up ones went into cooked tomato sauce, but the ripest and best were set aside for this amazing raw tomato sauce. It seems as though it might make a lot, but trust us—there won't be any leftovers!

8 large tomatoes (about 6 pounds)

Salt

1 teaspoon coarsely ground black pepper

1 teaspoon red pepper flakes

2 cups extra virgin olive oil

1 cup loosely packed basil leaves

2 pounds imported Italian fusilli pasta

⅓ pound Parmigiano-Reggiano cheese

WINE:
Planeta Rosé

SYRAH; MENFI, SICILY, ITALY

The fragrant acidity of this pomegranate- and floral-scented Syrah rosé agrees perfectly with fresh ripe tomatoes.

1. Core and seed the tomatoes. Turn each cored tomato upside down on several layers of paper towels and allow the excess juice to drain for 30 minutes. Cut each tomato into 6 to 8 slices, and then cut each slice into about 8 "cubes." In a large glass bowl, combine the tomatoes, 1 tablespoon salt, black pepper, pepper flakes, and oil. Cut the basil into strips with scissors, or tear by hand, and add to the bowl. Mix well with a wooden spoon. Cover with plastic wrap and let sit for a few hours. Do not refrigerate.

2. Bring 8 quarts water and 2 tablespoons salt to a rousing boil. Add the pasta and cook, stirring occasionally, according to package directions. (For al dente pasta, cook for about 1 minute less than recommended.) Drain.

3. Transfer the cooked pasta to a large serving platter. Top with the crudo sauce. Grate Parmigiano-Reggiano over the pasta using a Microplane.

PESTO-SMOTHERED GRILLED CHICKEN BREAST

MAKES 8 SERVINGS

The hot days of summer cause our garden to grow like wildfire. We usually have a bumper crop of basil. And what better way to use it, than to make delicious homemade pesto?

Pesto

¼ pound Romano cheese, cut into 1- to 2-inch chunks

2 cups loosely packed basil leaves

¼ cup pine nuts

2 cloves garlic, peeled

Juice of ½ lemon

¼ teaspoon ground black pepper

½ cup olive oil

Salt

Chicken

4 whole skinless, boneless chicken breasts, halved

¼ cup extra virgin olive oil

Juice of ½ lemon, plus lemon wedges for garnish

1 teaspoon salt

1 teaspoon ground black pepper

Whole basil leaves, for garnish

1. To make the pesto: Place the cheese in a food processor and process until coarsely grated. Add the basil, pine nuts, garlic, lemon juice, and pepper. Process to a thick paste, 45 seconds to 1 minute. Use a scraper to push down the sides. With the machine running, slowly drizzle in the oil through the feed tube until you have a thick liquid. Taste and add salt if needed. Transfer to an airtight container. Do not refrigerate if you plan on using the same day.

2. To prepare the chicken: Place the chicken in a glass baking dish and coat both sides with the oil, lemon juice, 2 tablespoons of the pesto, the salt, and pepper. Marinate in the refrigerator for at least 2 hours.

3. Preheat the grill. Grill the chicken for 5 to 7 minutes per side, depending on the thickness.

4. To serve, arrange the grilled chicken on a large serving platter. Spoon the remaining pesto over the entire platter. Garnish with lemon wedges and whole basil leaves.

WINE:

Carpineto Dogajolo Bianco

CHARDONNAY, GRECHETTO, AND SAUVIGNON BLANC; CHIANTI, TUSCANY, ITALY

A medium-bodied Chardonnay, Dogajolo complements the vibrant freshness of homemade pesto.

OR

St. Michael Eppan

PINOT BIANCO; ALTO ADIGE, ITALY

Smooth and slightly racy, this 100 percent Pinot Bianco from the foothills of the Italian Alps is ideal with this earthy pesto.

SALAD OF WILTED SPINACH, OIL-CURED BLACK OLIVES, AND BLOOD ORANGES

MAKES 8 SERVINGS

We enjoy our salads after the main course—just like the Italians! The warm dressing just barely wilts the spinach, and brings out its full flavor.

4 blood oranges

½ cup extra virgin olive oil

½ small red onion, cut into medium dice

2 cloves garlic, minced

1 teaspoon salt

1 teaspoon ground black pepper

Juice of 1 lemon

1 cup pitted oil-cured black olives

3 packages (8 ounces each) triple-washed baby spinach

Chunk of Parmesan cheese

1. Grate the zest from 1 of the blood oranges, then peel and section it. Peel and section 2 of the oranges. Slice the remaining orange to use for garnish.

2. Heat the oil in a large skillet. Add the onion, garlic, orange zest, salt, and pepper and cook until the garlic and onion soften. Add the lemon juice and olives. Stir until the olives are heated and well coated.

3. To serve, place the baby spinach on a large serving platter. Arrange the orange sections on top. Pour the heated olive mixture over the entire platter. Garnish with the orange slices. Shave some Parmesan on top and serve immediately.

WINE:
San Angelo Pinot Grigio

PINOT GRIGIO;
TUSCANY, ITALY

Straw-colored with a light fruity nose, this Pinot Grigio is well suited to the salad's citrus nature.

BASIL VANILLA ICE CREAM

MAKES 8 SERVINGS

One year for Mike's birthday, we stayed at a small château in Bordeaux, France, that had been turned into a hotel. We had a version of this ice cream at the hotel's Michelin-starred restaurant, and although we bought the chef's cookbook, we could never get his recipe to come out quite right. Mike experimented using a tried-and-true vanilla ice cream recipe, but because of the water in the basil, it kept turning icy. It took the addition of mascarpone to keep this from happening. This was back before the whole herbal and savory ice cream craze, so our Fire Island friends thought it was really strange when we first made it.

2 cups heavy cream

2 cups whole milk

3 tablespoons vanilla extract

8 egg yolks

1 cup sugar

3 cups loosely packed basil leaves (see Tip)

1 container (500 grams, about 1 pound) mascarpone

WINE:
Villa Rosa
Moscato d'Asti

MOSCATO; ASTI, PIEDMONT, ITALY

A mildly fizzy dessert wine made from 100 percent Moscato grapes is a wonderful finish to your night in Italy.

1. Combine the cream, milk, and 1 tablespoon of the vanilla in a heavy saucepan. Bring almost to a boil over medium heat, 6 to 9 minutes, then reduce the heat to low.

2. Beat together the egg yolks, sugar, and remaining 2 tablespoons vanilla in a bowl until smooth. Stir in ½ cup of the hot cream mixture until combined. Gradually add the egg yolk mixture to the remaining cream mixture in the saucepan, stirring constantly with a wooden spoon or wire whisk to prevent the eggs from curdling. Cook over low heat until slightly thickened and the mixture coats the back of a spoon. Set the custard aside.

(continued)

3. Wash and dry the basil leaves (see Tip). Place the basil and mascarpone in a food processor and process until smooth. Add 1 cup of the warm custard and process for about 30 seconds. Whisk the mascarpone-basil mixture back into the rest of the custard. Refrigerate for several hours (or quick-chill in an ice bath for 30 minutes).

4. Re-whisk the chilled mixture until well combined. Pour into the canister of an ice cream maker and freeze according to the manufacturer's instructions. Transfer the ice cream to an airtight container and freeze until firm, at least 2 hours. (May be made ahead of time and kept frozen until ready to serve.)

TIP: Make sure your basil is washed really well to get all the sand out. We rinse ours in a salad spinner, using several changes of water to ensure that it is thoroughly cleaned, and then spin until completely dry. Use only the leaves of the basil, discarding any that are badly wilted or discolored. Save a few of the leaves for garnish.

4

FOURTH OF JULY POOL PARTY

What all our memories of Independence Day have in common is time spent with family and friends, and easy food that can be eaten with the hands, or with just a fork, while standing around the pool, lounging on the sand or the grass, or perched on a wooden bench or folding chair with a plate in your lap and a smile on your face. We grew up eating hamburgers and hot dogs and maybe even fried chicken at summer picnics. And bowls of potato salad and coleslaw and a heaping platter of hot corn on the cob were always found atop the plastic-coated tablecloth as well. Lobster rolls now seem to be omnipresent in the Northeast, and this bit of New England is a welcome addition to our Fire Island summertime regime. All you need are a handful of sparklers, a red, white, and blue tablecloth, and a big bucket filled with ice and chilled wine to get you ready to head to the beach at sundown, tilt back your head, and let out a few oohs and aahs as the nighttime sky is illuminated and the sound of artificial thunder fills your ears.

BLUE CHEESE, BACON, AND FRIED ONION SLIDERS

LOBSTER ROLLS

OUR FAVORITE COLESLAW

RED, WHITE, AND BLUE POTATO SALAD

GRILLED CORN ON THE COB

STRAWBERRY-BLUEBERRY SHORTCAKE

For this picnic-style menu, you don't have to pair each course with a specific wine. Just have a big bucket of five or six different American wines—a couple of bubblies and a few whites and reds will satisfy everyone in your group. In keeping with our all-American theme, we've chosen some of our favorite red, white, and bubbly wines from California.

SPARKLING WINE:

Domaine Carneros Brut Rosé, Cuvée de la Pompadour by Taittinger

PINOT NOIR AND CHARDONNAY; CARNEROS, NAPA, CALIFORNIA

This elegant sparkler from California is named for Madame Pompadour, who said, "Champagne is the only wine that a woman can drink and remain beautiful."

Chandon Reserve Chardonnay Brut

CHARDONNAY; NAPA VALLEY, CALIFORNIA

What's the Fourth of July without a sparkler? This sparkling wine made from 100 percent Chardonnay grapes is a great way to start your meal, end your meal, or just drink straight through.

WHITE WINE:

Casa Dumetz Clementina Viognier

VIOGNIER, SANTA YNEZ VALLEY, CALIFORNIA

Kissed by the California sun, this French grape has delicate flavors of almond paste and rose petal with a decidedly bright finish.

Cakebread Cellars Sauvignon Blanc

SAUVIGNON BLANC; NAPA VALLEY, CALIFORNIA

Ripe melon and kiwi notes make this full-bodied Californian white a perfect choice for your backyard barbecue.

Villa San-Juliette Sauvignon Blanc

SAUVIGNON BLANC; PASO ROBLES, CALIFORNIA

"So You Think You Can Dance?" One sip of this fabulous wine will have you singing the praises of winery owner Nigel Lythgoe.

RED WINE:

St. Francis "Old Vines" Zinfandel

ZINFANDEL; SONOMA COUNTY, CALIFORNIA

Named for the Franciscan monks who brought grapes to America, this robust 100 percent Zin pairs perfectly with grilled meats.

Sequoia Grove Cabernet Sauvignon

CABERNET SAUVIGNON; NAPA VALLEY, CALIFORNIA

This well-proportioned Napa Valley Cab is marked by a balance between dark fruits and spice.

Hearst Ranch "Bunkhouse" Cabernet Sauvignon

CABERNET SAUVIGNON; PASO ROBLES, CALIFORNIA

With notes of red fruits, blueberry, and creamy vanilla, this stunning wine is an instant all-American classic.

BLUE CHEESE, BACON, AND FRIED ONION SLIDERS

MAKES 8 SERVINGS

If you were lucky (or unfortunate) enough to grow up near one of those hamburger stands that look like a miniature castle, you know the appeal of delicious small burgers. They are the perfect size to enjoy when you want the taste of a burger but don't want to fill up on just one thing. We don't cook ours on large griddles with steamed onions the way they do, but then again they don't give you the option of blue cheese and bacon toppings.

2 pounds ground sirloin

2 teaspoons salt

2 teaspoons ground black pepper

8 slices thick-cut bacon

2 large onions, cut into ½-inch-wide strips

8 teaspoons mayonnaise

16 slider buns or 4 regular hamburger buns, quartered

6 ounces crumbled blue cheese

1. Combine the beef, salt, and pepper and form sixteen 2-ounce patties.

2. In a large skillet, cook the bacon until crisp. Drain on paper towels. Add the onions to the bacon fat and cook until browned.

3. Preheat the grill to medium. Grill the burgers for 1½ to 2 minutes per side for medium-rare.

4. Spread ½ teaspoon mayonnaise on the bottom half of each bun. Top with a burger, fried onions, crumbled blue cheese, and a half slice of bacon. Cover with the top half of the bun and secure with a toothpick.

LOBSTER ROLLS

MAKES 8 SERVINGS

One time at our friend Julie's house on Cape Cod, we loaded a couple of boxes up with lobsters and settled in for a fun weekend of cooking. That evening we feasted on nothing but freshly steamed lobster with plenty of melted butter. Our eyes bigger than our stomachs, we had lots of lobster meat and butter left over, so we combined the two and put them in the refrigerator. The next day, we decided to make lobster rolls for lunch. We pulled the lobster out and were admonished by Julie for "ruining" the lobster meat by soaking it overnight in butter. It seems that a proper New Englander would make her sandwich only with lobster meat and mayonnaise— nothing more. Not ones to waste perfectly good food, we pulled the lobster out of the now hardened butter and tossed it with celery, salt, pepper, and mayonnaise. We toasted the buns in a little bit of fried butter and made the BEST lobster rolls any of us had EVER had. Our friends on Fire Island think so too!

4 live lobsters (2 pounds each)

Salt

8 tablespoons (1 stick) plus
    2 tablespoons salted butter

¾ cup mayonnaise

½ cup diced celery

1 teaspoon ground white pepper

8 hot dog buns

1. Get your hands on the largest pot you can find. Make sure the lobsters will fit comfortably in the pot with the lid firmly in place. Place the lobsters in the freezer while you add 2 inches of water and 1 tablespoon salt to the pot. Use a steaming rack if you have one; if not, don't worry. Bring the salted water to a rolling boil. Using tongs, quickly put the lobsters into the pot and secure the lid with a 5-pound weight. (Use a dumbbell or large juice can.) Steam the lobsters for 14 to 16 minutes. Remove the cooked lobsters from the pot and let cool.

2. In the microwave, melt
8 tablespoons of the butter in a glass
bowl. Crack the lobster claws and
tails. Pick out all of the meat and cut
into 1-inch chunks. Put the chunks
into the melted butter, toss well, and
refrigerate for at least 2 hours.

3. Combine the mayonnaise, celery,
1 teaspoon salt, the pepper, and the
lobster in a large glass bowl. Toss
until well coated.

4. Using the remaining 2 tablespoons
butter, lightly butter the insides
of the hot dog buns and toast in a
skillet until golden brown. Spoon
equal amounts of the lobster salad
into each and serve.

OUR FAVORITE COLESLAW

MAKES 8 SERVINGS

Made from cabbage and carrots, this crunchy salad is crisp, colorful, and an excellent side dish for your Fourth of July pool party.

I large head red cabbage

4 large carrots

I cup mayonnaise

⅓ cup distilled white vinegar

¼ cup sugar

2 teaspoons salt

I teaspoon coarsely ground black pepper

I teaspoon caraway seeds

1. Using a large holed grater, a mandoline, or a food processor with the slicing disk, grate the cabbage and carrots.

2. Whisk together the mayonnaise, vinegar, sugar, salt, pepper, and caraway seeds in a large glass bowl. Add the grated cabbage and carrots and toss well. Refrigerate for 2 hours, tossing occasionally to blend the flavors. Transfer to a clean bowl to serve.

RED, WHITE, AND BLUE POTATO SALAD

MAKES 8 SERVINGS

Even the strictest "carb counters" can't resist this delicious *and* beautiful potato salad. Use small thin-skinned potatoes—and leave the peels on. If all the potatoes are about the same size, the dish looks much better.

1½ pounds small red potatoes, quartered

1½ pounds small white potatoes, quartered

1 pound small blue potatoes, quartered

Salt

1 cup mayonnaise

¼ cup distilled white vinegar

1 teaspoon dry mustard

1 tablespoon ground white pepper

2 medium red onions, finely diced

1. Combine the potatoes in a large pot with 8 quarts cold water and 1 tablespoon salt. Bring the water to a rolling boil and cook until the potato chunks are tender, about 12 minutes. Do not overcook. Drain in a colander and rinse with cold water. Set aside while you make the dressing.

2. Whisk together the mayonnaise, vinegar, mustard, 4 teaspoons salt, and the pepper in a large glass bowl. Add the potatoes and onions and toss until everything is well coated. Transfer to a serving bowl and refrigerate for at least 2 hours.

GRILLED CORN ON THE COB

MAKES 8 SERVINGS

Although we both always had boiled corn while growing up, grilled corn is now a staple at street fairs, country fairs—and Fourth of July barbecues!

8 ears freshly picked local corn

1 tablespoon fine sea salt

8 tablespoons (1 stick) butter, melted

1. Shuck the corn carefully by pulling the husks down from top to bottom toward the stalk. Be careful not to rip the husks off. Remove the silk from each ear and return the husks to their original position. To hold the husks in place, take any husks that have accidentally fallen off and tie one around each ear. In a large pot, stir the salt into 8 quarts cold water. Add the corn and soak for 1 hour.

2. Let the corn drain while you preheat the grill to medium.

3. Grill the husk-covered ears of corn for 8 to 12 minutes.

4. To serve, peel back the husks and tie them together at the bottom to create a large "handle" to hold the corn. Brush each ear with butter.

STRAWBERRY-BLUEBERRY SHORTCAKE

MAKES 8 SERVINGS

One Fourth of July, we were inspired by our friend Tammy's strawberry shortcake. Unable to beg or threaten her secret recipe out of her, we played around in the kitchen until we were able to come up with our own. Now, she's the one doing the begging. We also decided to make ours more all-American by bringing out the red, white, and blue with the addition of fresh-picked New Jersey blueberries.

Berries

2 pints strawberries

2 pints blueberries

½ cup sugar

Grated zest of 1 lemon

Shortcakes

2 cups all-purpose flour

2 teaspoons baking powder

½ teaspoon baking soda

¾ teaspoon salt

2 tablespoons sugar

8 tablespoons (1 stick) cold butter, cut into chunks

¾ cup heavy cream

Topping

2 cups heavy cream

½ cup confectioners' sugar

1. Prepare the berries: Wash the berries in cold tap water and let drain. Hull and slice the strawberries. Combine the blueberries, strawberries, sugar, and lemon zest in a glass bowl. Toss and set aside for 2 hours.

2. Meanwhile, make the shortcakes: Preheat the oven to 400°F.

3. Combine the flour, baking powder, baking soda, salt, and sugar in a large bowl. Using your hands, combine the butter with the flour mixture until you have coarse pebbles. Slowly add the cream and mix with a wooden spoon until everything is combined and you are able to form a ball. Divide into 8 equal pieces and gently work the dough into small flattened balls. Bake on a nonstick baking sheet until the tops are golden brown, 13 to 16 minutes. Transfer to a rack to cool.

(continued)

4. To make the topping: Put a bowl and beaters into the freezer for 30 minutes. Place the cream in the cold bowl and whip at medium speed for 2 minutes. Add the confectioners' sugar slowly and continue whipping until stiff peaks form. Do not overwhip.

5. To assemble: Split the shortcakes horizontally. Place the bottom half on a dessert plate. Spoon 3 to 4 tablespoons of the strawberry and blueberry mixture onto each. Liberally top each with whipped cream and top with the other half of the shortcake. Serve immediately and enjoy.

5

NEPTUNE'S BOUNTY

Neptune, the Roman god of the sea, is a symbol of not only the ocean, but also the wonderful fish we eat all season long. Even at the end of the hottest summer day, a dinner of seafood feels fresh and light. With a little bit of planning, you can spend the best hours of daylight at the beach and still have this meal on the table in record time. The shrimp and pineapple skewers can be set up in advance, as can the niçoise salad; and if you chop your onions and scallions early in the day, the bouillabaisse can simmer while you enjoy the first two courses.

Every beach town has at least one good fish market, and there is something so refreshing about stepping inside a cold shop with a tile floor and ice everywhere. We like to go early in the day, and if we're not heading straight home, we always bring a cooler along to keep our "catch" cold. On Fire Island, where cars aren't allowed, that means pulling the cooler in a little red wagon. If you have a choice, get shrimp that are already cleaned—they cost a little bit more but are well worth it in the time-saving department, especially when your time could be much better spent ducking under waves or curling up in the shade of a striped umbrella with a dog-eared best-seller and a glass of ice-cold white wine.

GRILLED SPICY SHRIMP AND PINEAPPLE SKEWERS
WINE: *Santiago Ruiz*

SEARED TUNA NIÇOISE SALAD
WINE: *Domaine Des Victoires Quincy*

BOUILLABAISSE
WINE: *Jean-Luc Colombo Cape Bleue Rosé or Château Beaulieu Rosé*

TANGERINE-MINT PROSECCO SORBET
WINE: *Villa Sandi Prosecco*

GRILLED SPICY SHRIMP AND PINEAPPLE SKEWERS

MAKES 8 SERVINGS

We first had shrimp and pineapple skewers at a tapas bar in Logroño, the capital of the Rioja wine region. We often go out on a "tapas crawl" rather than sitting down for a formal dinner. Our movable feast usually involves four or five tapas bars, each one offering its special tapas served alongside amazing wines by the glass. After a few glasses, it's hard to remember the names of all the bars we visited, but we can tell you that the one that makes the best pineapple and shrimp skewers is down the street from the small alleyway that connects the two main streets and is only a few blocks behind the cathedral, or was it the town hall? Anyway, come with us next time and we will show you.

24 extra-large or 32 large shrimp (about 1¼ pounds)

⅓ cup olive oil

1½ tablespoons paprika

1 teaspoon red pepper flakes

2 teaspoons salt

1 large pineapple

4 limes, quartered, for garnish

WINE:
Santiago Ruiz

ALBARIÑO BLEND; RIAS BAIXAS, GALICIA, SPAIN

A harmonious mélange of citrus flavors with well-tempered minerality partners well with the salinity and fruit of the spicy shrimp and pineapple skewers.

1. In a pitcher or tall pot, soak ten 12-inch wooden skewers in water for several hours. This will minimize the burning. You will use only 8 of them, but they sometimes splinter, so it's good to soak a few extras to be safe.

2. Clean and devein the shrimp, and remove the tails. (Or buy shrimp that have already been cleaned.) Stir together the oil, paprika, pepper flakes, and salt in a glass bowl. Add the shrimp and lightly toss until well coated.

3. Quarter, core, and peel the pineapple. Cut each quarter wedge crosswise into 8 slices about 1 inch thick.

4. Run skewers through the shrimp and pineapple pieces, alternating one shrimp with one piece of pineapple. If using extra-large shrimp, you will have 3 shrimp per skewer; with large, there will be 4 per skewer. As you work, the shrimp marinade will coat the pineapple, too.

5. Tear off 4 lengths of foil about 3 inches wide. Cut each strip into 4 pieces, and wrap the exposed ends of the skewers in foil to prevent burning or catching fire.

6. Preheat the grill to medium. Using tongs, lay the skewers across the grill and grill until the shrimp turn pink and begin to curl, 2 to 3 minutes per side.

7. Transfer to a platter (see Tip) as they're done and garnish with lime wedges. Make sure your guests have a knife and fork to slide the shrimp and pineapple off the skewer and onto their plates.

TIP: Before starting, cover a platter large enough to hold all the skewers with 2 or 3 layers of plastic wrap. Lay the uncooked skewers on this platter, and when you transfer them to the grill, simply remove and discard the plastic wrap. You now have a clean platter on which to place the cooked shrimp and pineapple when done!

SEARED TUNA NIÇOISE SALAD

Although *salade niçoise* is usually made with canned tuna, we have updated the classic with barely cooked sushi-grade tuna. You can prepare most of this course before your guests arrive, plate the salad, and then take a few minutes to sear the tuna just prior to serving. We have also prepared this completely in advance, allowing the tuna to cool before plating, and placed all the dishes in the refrigerator, ready to serve. This allows us to relax with our guests during dinner.

4 eggs

⅓ cup extra virgin olive oil, plus extra for cooking the tuna

I tablespoon red wine vinegar

I tablespoon fresh lemon juice

I teaspoon Dijon mustard

¼ teaspoon ground black pepper

I pound mesclun

I cup mixed green and black olives

Half a 15.5-ounce can chickpeas, drained

2 cans (2 ounces each) anchovy fillets

1½ pounds sushi-grade tuna (2 to 3 steaks)

Salt

¼ cup capers, drained

1. Place the eggs in a small saucepan with water to cover. Bring to a boil over medium heat, turn off the heat, cover, and let stand for 15 minutes. Hold the eggs under cold running water until cool enough to handle. Peel, dry with a paper towel, and set aside.

2. In a glass measuring cup, whisk together ⅓ cup oil and the vinegar, lemon juice, mustard, and pepper.

3. Arrange the mesclun on 8 salad plates, rewhisk the dressing, and pour evenly over the greens. Quarter the hard-boiled eggs lengthwise. Around the edges of each plate, arrange 2 egg quarters, a few olives, and a few chickpeas. Remove the anchovies from the can, separate, and lay out on a small plate.

(continued)

WINE:

*Domaine Des
Victoires Quincy*

SAUVIGNON BLANC;
QUINCY, LOIRE, FRANCE

The Loire Valley produces some
fine examples of Sauvignon Blanc;
this is one of them.

4. Cut the tuna steaks lengthwise into 2 to 3 strips, 2½ to 3 inches wide. Sprinkle the tuna lightly with salt and pepper. Preheat a cast-iron skillet over high heat. Reduce the heat slightly and pour in a small amount of olive oil. Working quickly so you don't burn your fingers, spread the oil over the bottom of the pan with a bunched paper towel. Using tongs, place the tuna in the pan and cook for 1½ minutes per side. If the tuna is more than 2 inches thick, quickly sear the sides as well. Transfer to a large cutting board and cut into ¼-inch-thick slices.

5. Arrange a few slices of seared tuna in the center of each mound of salad. Cross 2 anchovies in the shape of an X over the tuna slices, and sprinkle a few capers onto the tuna. Serve immediately.

BOUILLABAISSE

MAKES 8 SERVINGS

Anybody who studied French in high school can tell you that *bouillabaisse* is a fancy way of saying fish chowder. Although it usually consists of Mediterranean varieties of fish such as conger eel, scorpion fish, bream, and monkfish, our adaptation of this French favorite uses seafood and shellfish available on Fire Island and the whole Eastern seaboard, which are more suited to American palates.

3 tablespoons extra virgin olive oil

3 large Spanish onions, sliced

2 medium red onions, sliced

3 bunches scallions, sliced

6 cloves garlic, sliced

3 large tomatoes, cut into ½-inch cubes

I tablespoon salt

I tablespoon coarsely ground black pepper

4 cups bottled clam juice

3 bay leaves

½ teaspoon aniseed

½ teaspoon dried thyme

2 pounds mussels (see Tip)

2 pounds clams (see Tip)

2 pounds large shrimp, peeled and deveined

I pound bay scallops

I pound sea scallops

2 lemons, I squeezed and both zested

2 loaves crusty French bread, for serving

1. Heat the oil in a large, heavy-bottomed pot. Add the onions, scallions, and garlic to the pot and cook until soft, about 5 minutes. Add the tomatoes, salt, and pepper. Cook for 5 minutes, then add the clam juice and 8 cups water. Add the bay leaves, aniseed, and thyme. Bring to a boil, then reduce to a low simmer, cover, and cook for about 30 minutes.

2. Add the mussels and clams and bring to a boil again, reduce the heat to a medium simmer, cover, and cook until the clams and mussels open up, about 10 minutes.

3. Mixing gently, add the shrimp, bay scallops, and sea scallops, and cook, covered, for 5 minutes. Do not overcook. Remove from the heat and add the lemon juice and zest and gently mix again.

(continued)

63

WINE:

Jean-Luc Colombo Cape Bleue Rosé

SYRAH, MOURVÈDRE, AND
COUNOISE; COTEAUX D'AIX-EN-
PROVENCE, PROVENCE, FRANCE

This raspberry-, black olive–, and fennel-scented rosé is from the hills just above Marseilles, the home of bouillabaisse.

OR

Château Beaulieu Rosé

GRENACHE, CABERNET SAUVIGNON,
AND SYRAH; COTEAUX D'AIX-EN-
PROVENCE, PROVENCE, FRANCE

Located in a volcanic crater, with some of the best soils for grape growing, Château Beaulieu produces one of the finest rosés in the region.

4. To serve, ladle the bouillabaisse into large shallow soup bowls. Serve with the French bread to sop up the broth. And remember to have bowls on the table for your guests to discard their shells.

TIP: To clean clams and mussels, place them in a large bowl filled with cold water. Let sit for 10 minutes, tip the bowl back and forth a few times, then change the water. Repeat three times. This allows the shellfish to release any sand that they may have stored.

TANGERINE-MINT PROSECCO SORBET

MAKES 8 SERVINGS

Not far from our home in southern Spain, we can take a high-speed ferry across the Strait of Gibraltar to Tangier, on the north coast of Morocco. Although there are orange trees in almost every village square on the Costa del Sol, the oranges are bitter, unsuitable for anything but the making of preserves. The tangerine trees in Tangier, however, bear fruit that is full of sweetness and ready to eat upon picking. Tangerines and cups of sugared mint tea are offered by shopkeepers while carpets are unfurled across marble floors, or while customers wait for henna designs to dry on thin leather lampshades. These two flavors of North Africa blend perfectly with the citrus and honey tones of prosecco, the sparkling wine from the north of Italy.

3 cups tangerine sections

½ cup sugar

12 mint leaves

1½ cups prosecco

3 tablespoons fresh lemon juice

⅛ teaspoon salt

WINE:
Villa Sandi Prosecco

PROSECCO; TREVISO, VENETO, ITALY

Lightly *frizzante* and citrus-scented Villa Sandi Prosecco is a wonderful way to finish your meal.

Place the tangerine sections, sugar, and mint leaves in a medium stainless steel bowl that fits comfortably over a saucepan to function as a double boiler. Bring water to a simmer in the saucepan. Mash the tangerines, mint leaves, and sugar together and place over the simmering water. Continue mashing until the sugar melts. Remove from the heat and let cool. When cool, place in a food processor and pulse into coarse chunks. Do not overprocess. Add the prosecco, lemon juice, and salt and mix well. Refrigerate until cold. When cold, transfer to an ice cream maker and freeze according to the manufacturer's instructions. Enjoy.

6

MYKONOS BY TORCHLIGHT

Late-night summer dinners are really the best. After a full day of swimming and body-surfing, you almost feel that you're on a boat, and the hypnotic sound of crashing waves adds to the romance of the evening. Add a few well-placed torches around the deck, and you could be on an exotic island in the Aegean. But you're not—you're here at the beach, with your family and friends, enjoying a fun, easy-to-make meal.

In this Greek-inspired menu, the first two dishes and dessert are served cold. So is the caponata that accompanies the lamb—and even the lamb is marinated ahead of time and finished on the grill. So go ahead and watch the sun set over the Great South Bay. As wonderful as it will be, dinner can wait.

FETA CHEESE BAKED IN PUFF PASTRY
WINE: *Boutari Santorini*

TOMATO, CUCUMBER, AND FETA SALAD
WINE: *Gerovassiliou Malagousia*

ROSEMARY-RUBBED BONELESS LEG OF LAMB WITH TOMATO-EGGPLANT CAPONATA
WINE: *Biblia Chora Estate, Red or Boutari Naoussa*

PISTACHIO FROZEN GREEK YOGURT
WINE: *Sigalas Vin Santo*

FETA CHEESE BAKED IN PUFF PASTRY

MAKES 8 SERVINGS

Jeff just can't get enough of these delightful feta cheese pastry bites. Anytime we pass a bakery in Greece, whether we're on foot, in a car, or even late for an appointment, the scent of feta cheese baking lifts and carries him like a cartoon wolf floating on the scent of grilled lamb chops. In Greece, these are traditionally made using phyllo dough, but we prefer the buttery, flaky goodness that puff pastry adds to the taste and mouthfeel of these delectable morsels.

½ pound imported Greek feta cheese, crumbled

2 tablespoons finely chopped chives

1 tablespoon finely chopped parsley

⅛ teaspoon ground nutmeg

1 egg, beaten, plus 1 egg yolk

1 package (12 ounces) good-quality frozen puff pastry, thawed

Ice water

WINE:
Boutari Santorini

ASSYRTIKO; SANTORINI, GREECE

Made from Assyrtiko, the signature grape of Santorini, this vibrant wine has notes of melon and peach.

1. Combine the cheese, chives, parsley, nutmeg, and beaten egg in a medium glass bowl. Set the filling aside.

2. Preheat the oven to 400°F.

3. Lay out the pastry on a lightly floured surface and cut into sixteen 3-inch squares. Beat the egg yolk with 2 teaspoons water.

4. Place a heaping teaspoon of the feta filling in the center of each square. Using your fingertips, wet all of the edges of the square with ice water. Fold over to form a triangle. Seal the edges using the tines of a fork and brush each triangle with the beaten egg yolk.

5. Place on a baking sheet and bake until golden brown, 20 to 23 minutes. Let cool on a rack for 15 minutes.

TOMATO, CUCUMBER, AND FETA SALAD

MAKES 8 SERVINGS

There's nothing simpler and more delicious than a fresh Greek salad. Contrary to what many New York City diners and restaurants try to pass off as a real Greek salad, the original has only three (or four, if you use onion) key ingredients. The trick to this delicious starter is using only the best-quality olive oil and the ripest tomatoes.

8 medium tomatoes, seeded and cut into 1-inch chunks

6 cucumbers, seeded and cut into 1-inch chunks

½ cup extra virgin olive oil

Juice of 1 lemon, plus lemon wedges for garnish

1 teaspoon salt

1 teaspoon coarsely ground black pepper

¾ pound imported Greek feta cheese

Oregano leaves, for garnish

Combine the tomatoes and cucumbers in a glass bowl. Add the oil, lemon juice, salt, and pepper and toss well. Crumble the feta cheese on top and toss lightly, so as not to break the feta down any further. Cover with plastic wrap and set aside. Serve in small bowls and garnish with lemon wedges and oregano leaves.

WINE:
Gerovassiliou Malagousia

MALAGOUSIA; THESSALONIKI, GREECE

This expressive white wine blends together citrus and herbal notes, which harmonize ideally with this fresh summer salad.

ROSEMARY-RUBBED BONELESS LEG OF LAMB WITH TOMATO-EGGPLANT CAPONATA

MAKES 8 SERVINGS

All across southern Europe, rosemary grows wild. In the regional soil, it blossoms into bushes the size of cars. Rosemary also pushes its way through craggy hillside rocks, where it remains untouched, except by slightly insane hikers (like us, whose legs it scratches) and by migrating herds of sheep, who feed upon it as they pass. Mediterranean lamb tastes as if it were marinated in rosemary even if it is only dusted with salt and pepper, but we prefer to gild the lily and add a little more to the outside before placing it on the grill.

8 sprigs fresh rosemary

2 cloves garlic, finely slivered

¼ cup coarse salt

2 tablespoons coarsely ground black pepper

½ cup extra virgin olive oil

3 tablespoons fresh lemon juice

1 small boneless leg of lamb (3½ to 4 pounds)

Tomato-Eggplant Caponata (page 76: see Tip below)

1. Remove the rosemary leaves from the stems and place the leaves in a mortar and pestle. Add the garlic, salt, and pepper and grind together until the rosemary begins to break down and release its oils. Transfer to a small bowl and stir in the oil and lemon juice.

2. Cut the leg of lamb in half through the center, creating two steaks about 2 to 2½ inches thick. Rub both sides of the lamb steaks with the rosemary mixture and let rest at least 2 hours in the refrigerator before grilling.

3. Preheat the grill to high. Grill the lamb for 8 to 10 minutes per side for medium-rare. Slice and serve with a portion of the caponata on the side.

TIP: Caponata tastes best when it is made in advance and the flavors have time to meld together. This can be made 1 to 2 days before serving, or make it early in the morning before heading to the beach.

WINE:

Biblia Chora Estate, Red

CABERNET SAUVIGNON AND
MERLOT; KAVALA, GREECE

Garnet-colored with ripe red
fruit followed by a spicy finish,
Biblia Chora matches the intensity
of the caponata's spice and the
earthiness of succulent lamb.

OR

Boutari Naoussa

XINOMAVRO;
NAOUSSA, GREECE

Full-bodied red with notes of
berries and vanilla. Historically, this
was the first bottled wine available
in Greece, but it's certainly not
your grandfather's wine.

TOMATO-EGGPLANT CAPONATA

MAKES 8 SERVINGS

This is a version of a Sicilian dish that Mike's grandmother, Paolina DiBella Termini, always made for holidays. His family called it *caponatina*, or "little caponata." It was usually served with the *antipasti*, but it is a delicious side dish as well. Growing up, Mike always corrected people if they said he was "Italian," as he is 100 percent Sicilian. Travel has taught him that the food of Sicily has much more in common with Greek cuisine than with typical Italian-American fare.

2 medium to large eggplants
(about 2 pounds)

Salt

Olive oil

1 large red onion, diced

3 plum tomatoes, diced

2 stalks celery, halved lengthwise
and thinly sliced

1 can (6 ounces) tomato paste

2 tablespoons red wine vinegar

1 teaspoon sugar

½ teaspoon ground black pepper

½ teaspoon dried oregano

⅛ teaspoon ground cinnamon

⅓ cup capers, drained

¼ cup pine nuts

1. Remove the ends from the eggplants and quarter lengthwise. Cut each quarter into about 8 wedges and stand skin side down on a baking sheet lined with paper towels. Sprinkle with salt and let stand for 1 hour, until excess water drains from the eggplant.

2. Preheat the oven to 350°F. Transfer the eggplant to a clean baking sheet, brush with oil, and roast for 20 minutes, until slightly browned.

3. In a large, high-sided skillet, heat ¼ cup oil over high heat. Add the onion, salt lightly, and cook until wilted. Reduce the heat to medium and add the plum tomatoes, celery, and roasted eggplant, stirring with a wooden spoon. If the eggplant soaks up all of the oil, move your ingredients to the sides of the pan and add 2 more tablespoons oil. Stir until you can cut the larger pieces of eggplant in half with the edge of a wooden spoon, about 5 minutes. When the eggplant is sufficiently softened, stir in the tomato paste, vinegar, 1 teaspoon salt, the sugar, pepper, oregano, and cinnamon. Reduce the heat to low and stir in the capers and pine nuts. Simmer, covered, stirring occasionally, until the eggplant begins to break down, about 20 minutes. Transfer to a glass container and refrigerate until ready to serve.

PISTACHIO FROZEN GREEK YOGURT

MAKES 8 SERVINGS

Mike loves pistachio nuts—in fact he collects them. No matter what Mediterranean country we visit, he has to traipse through each and every spice market to find them. It sounds crazy, but one day he conducted his very own private tasting. He set out five bowls filled with pistachios from Spain, Greece, Italy, Sicily, and Turkey to determine which were the best. After two hours of chomping, munching, and note taking, his findings were inconclusive, but he certainly had a lot of fun.

It's sad but true that frozen yogurt is better for us than ice cream. In fact, the Greeks eat very little ice cream, yet most eat yogurt every day—that could be the reason they live so long. Here's a recipe that's easy to make, uses Mike's favorite snack, is healthy for your guests, and doesn't compromise on taste.

¾ cup sugar

3 cups good-quality Greek yogurt

1½ teaspoons almond extract

¼ cup chopped pistachio nuts plus ¼ cup whole pistachios

WINE:

Sigalas Vin Santo

ASSYRTIKO AND AIDANI;
SANTORINI, GREECE

This sun-kissed, sweet wine from Santorini is like a glass of liquefied honey touched by the hand of Zeus.

1. Whisk the sugar into the yogurt in a glass bowl. Add the almond extract and the chopped and whole pistachios, and mix well. Refrigerate for 2 hours.

2. Transfer the mixture to the canister of an ice cream maker and freeze according to the manufacturer's instructions. Serve immediately, or return to the freezer until ready to serve.

7

PORTSIDE IN PUERTO VALLARTA

Warm weather makes us think of Mexican food—jalapeños and habaneros seem so right in summer. Spicy, simply prepared food is ideal as the sky turns dark and the air chills down just a touch. And although soup in the summertime is almost counterintuitive, a dish that is high both in temperature and on the Scoville scale makes you and everyone else feel a little bit cooler.

We are big fans of food that can be made in advance, but guacamole isn't one of those, as avocados start to discolor as soon as they are cut and exposed to air. Have all your other dishes ready to go, then mix up a pitcher of margaritas, put your friends and family to work chopping and dicing, and let your fiesta begin at the kitchen counter. Olé!

HAND-MASHED GUACAMOLE

HOME-FRIED TORTILLA CHIPS

COCKTAIL: *Cazadores Reposado Tequila and Cointreau Margarita*

MAYAN CHICKEN AND LIME SOUP

WINE: *Santa Rita 120*

TEQUILA-MARINATED HANGER STEAK ON A BED OF GRILLED PEPPERS AND ONIONS

WINE: *Catena Malbec or Cousiño-Macul*

VANILLA HABANERO ICE CREAM WITH CAJETA

DIGESTIVE: *Don Roberto Añejo Tequila*

HAND-MASHED GUACAMOLE

MAKES 8 SERVINGS

We love hand-mashed guacamole and often make it at home with our friends. Ian cuts the onions, Cris dices the tomatoes, Sue washes and chops the cilantro, and Lucy is the best avocado masher we know. Avocados originated in Mexico and were held in high esteem by the Aztecs.

4 avocados

3 plum tomatoes, finely diced

3 tablespoons chopped fresh cilantro

I small red onion, finely diced

2 limes

I teaspoon Tabasco sauce

I teaspoon salt

½ teaspoon ground black pepper

Halve the avocados lengthwise, remove the pit, and scoop the flesh into a glass bowl. Add the tomatoes, cilantro, and onion. Squeeze the limes into a small sieve and add the juice to the bowl along with the Tabasco, salt, and pepper. Using a large-tined fork, mash the contents of the bowl into a medium- to large-chunked guacamole. Serve immediately.

COCKTAIL:

Cazadores Reposado Tequila and Cointreau Margarita

Nothing goes better with guacamole than a freshly mixed margarita (page 83) on the rocks, stirred and not shaken—sorry, Mr. Bond.

HOME-FRIED TORTILLA CHIPS

MAKES 8 SERVINGS

There is really nothing easier than frying your own tortilla chips. But if you don't have either time or a deep-fryer, good-quality chips can be purchased almost anywhere.

Vegetable oil, for deep-frying

16 corn tortillas, cut into
    6 wedges each

Sea salt

In a deep skillet, heat 2 inches of oil over high heat. (Or heat the oil in a deep-fryer.) Fry 10 to 12 tortilla wedges at a time. When golden brown, remove with a slotted spoon and place on paper towels to drain. Sprinkle with sea salt and serve.

MARGARITAS

MAKES 8 SERVINGS

To rim a margarita glass, cover the bottom of a small plate with coarse salt. Put a little bit of water in another small plate or bowl, and dip the rim of each glass first into the water and then into the salt. When filling, be careful to pour into the center of the glass so you don't "knock" the salt off.

16 ounces Cazadores Tequila Reposado

8 ounces Cointreau

8 ounces fresh lime juice

3 ounces agave nectar

Coarse salt, for rimming the glasses

2 limes, cut into wedges

Mix all the ingredients in a big glass pitcher filled with ice. Stir well with a wooden spoon. Pour into 8 glasses that have been rimmed with coarse salt, filled with ice, and garnished with a lime wedge. *¡Salud!*

MAYAN CHICKEN AND LIME SOUP

MAKES 8 SERVINGS

So there we are, exploring this rarely visited and deserted (and we mean *deserted*) Mayan ruin and we hear this low growl. We both stop, each thinking that the other made the noise, only to hear, *loud* this time, a second growl. Not waiting to figure out what it was, we both turned on our heels and ran back to the jeep like scared children. While the waiter placed this soup in front of us that evening, he told us the story of how the ancient Mayans believed that jaguars guarded their temples from intruders. Hmmmmm . . .

2 cups long-grain rice

¼ cup olive oil

12 cloves garlic, thinly sliced

2 medium Spanish onions, diced

Salt and ground black pepper

4 jalapeño peppers, seeded and thinly sliced

8 skin-on, bone-in chicken thighs

12 cups chicken stock

2 large tomatoes, seeded and chopped

⅔ cup finely chopped fresh cilantro, plus cilantro sprigs for garnish

⅔ cup fresh lime juice

Tortilla chips, for garnish

1. Cook the rice according to package directions. Set aside.

2. Preheat a large saucepan over medium heat. Add the oil and heat until it sizzles. Add the garlic and onions, season lightly with salt and pepper, and cook until soft and golden. Stir in the jalapeños. Move the onions, jalapeños, and garlic to the perimeter and add the chicken thighs skin side down. Cook for 5 minutes. Add the chicken stock and tomatoes. Bring to a boil, then reduce to a simmer, cover, and cook for 1 hour, stirring occasionally.

3. Remove the chicken with tongs. When cool enough to handle, shred the meat with your fingers and a fork. Discard the skin and bones. Add the shredded chicken back to the soup and simmer for 10 minutes. Remove from the heat and stir in the chopped cilantro and lime juice.

WINE:

Santa Rita 120

SAUVIGNON BLANC; CENTRAL VALLEY, CHILE

This wine is named for the 120 patriots who helped lead Chile to independence. The herbaceous and citrus character of this Southern Hemisphere Sauvignon Blanc teams impeccably with the lime and cilantro in our Mayan chicken soup.

4. To serve, divide the rice among 8 bowls and ladle the soup over it. Garnish with cilantro sprigs and tortilla chips.

TEQUILA-MARINATED HANGER STEAK ON A BED OF GRILLED PEPPERS AND ONIONS

MAKES 8 SERVINGS

We'll never forget the first time we had this delicious steak. Exhausted and starving, we stopped at a roadside taco stand on the outskirts of Puerto Vallarta and could not believe how tender and juicy the meat was. The four-foot-tall, gold-toothed cook told us her secret ingredient: tequila.

Steaks and marinade

½ cup white tequila

¼ cup fresh lime juice

1 tablespoon coarse salt

1 tablespoon coarsely ground black pepper

1 tablespoon sugar

2 dried habanero peppers, crumbled

2 hanger steaks (2 pounds each)

Peppers and onions

6 large red bell peppers, cut into ½-inch-wide strips

6 green bell peppers, cut into ½-inch-wide strips

8 medium onions, cut into ½-inch-wide strips

2 tablespoons extra virgin olive oil

1 teaspoon salt

1 teaspoon ground black pepper

1. To prepare the steak: Combine the tequila, lime juice, salt, black pepper, sugar, and habaneros in a large resealable plastic bag and shake until well mixed. Add the steaks and shake again. Make sure that both steaks are well coated with marinade. Refrigerate for 8 hours.

2. Meanwhile, to make the peppers and onions: Preheat the grill to low to medium. Lay a double layer of 3-foot-long heavy-duty foil on your counter. Place the bell peppers and onions in the center and sprinkle with the oil, salt, and black pepper. Fold the ends of the foil to the center to create a foil pouch and seal all loose ends. Poke 2 or 3 fork holes in the top and place on the grill until softened, about 15 minutes.

(continued)

WINE:

Catena Malbec

MALBEC; MENDOZA, ARGENTINA

The Catena Winery in Mendoza is a loving re-creation of an Aztec temple. Its intense Malbec is a worthy partner for this succulent steak.

OR

Cousiño-Macul

CABERNET SAUVIGNON; MAIPO, CENTRAL VALLEY, CHILE

Fermented in 100 percent stainless steel, this sumptuous Cabernet retains the true fruit character of the grape.

3. When ready to cook the steak, preheat the grill to high for 10 minutes. Reduce the heat to medium and grill the steaks 4 to 5 minutes on each side for medium-rare. Cut each steak into 4 equal portions.

4. To serve, place a heaping scoop of the grilled vegetables in the center of a dinner plate and top with the steak.

VANILLA HABANERO ICE CREAM WITH CAJETA

MAKES 8 SERVINGS

When you get an ice cream maker, the first flavor you make is the simplest and most delicious—vanilla. When Mike got his, he was on a "hot streak," and was experimenting with different types of peppers in everything he cooked. The dried habanero adds a hot, smoky kick to the ice cream, but the dairy fat will put out the fire in your mouth.

10 large egg yolks

1 cup sugar

2 cups whole milk

2 cups heavy cream

2 dried habanero peppers

Cajeta (page 91)

DIGESTIVE:
Don Roberto Añejo Tequila

TEQUILA, JALISCO, MEXICO

With notes of deep spice, toasted vanilla bean, and caramel, Don Roberto Añejo Tequila and Vanilla Habanero Ice Cream with Cajeta are surely twins separated at birth. Enjoy the tequila in your favorite brandy snifter.

1. Whisk the egg yolks and sugar together in a glass bowl until creamy.

2. Combine the milk, cream, and habaneros in a heavy-bottomed saucepan. Bring to a boil, stirring frequently with a wooden spoon. Using a ½-cup measure or a large spoon, gradually add the hot milk mixture to the eggs and sugar, stirring constantly. Return the mixture to the saucepan and stir over medium heat until the custard is thick enough to coat the back of a spoon, 10 to 15 minutes. Do not boil.

3. Pour the custard into a glass bowl. Using small tongs or a slotted spoon, remove the habaneros. (If they have broken apart during cooking, pour the custard through a fine-mesh sieve to remove any seeds or bits of pepper.) Let cool to room temperature, then refrigerate for 2 to 24 hours to chill before making into ice cream.

(continued)

4. Pour into the canister of an ice cream maker and freeze according to the manufacturer's instructions. Transfer to a covered plastic container and place in the freezer.

5. To serve, use an ice cream scoop and place one ball (or two—why not?) of ice cream in a small bowl. Top with *cajeta*. If the *cajeta* has hardened too much to pour over the ice cream, simply heat it again for a few minutes. Enjoy!

CAJETA

MAKES 8 SERVINGS

If you've ever read Gabriel García Márquez's *One Hundred Years of Solitude,* you know that the Buendia family women kept the children of Macondo happy by plying them with *cajeta* lollipops. As you may have figured out, we love anything caramel, and *cajeta* is one of the most delicious permutations, made with fresh goat's milk.

2 cups sugar

¼ teaspoon salt

2 tablespoons unsalted butter

½ cup goat's milk

Combine the sugar and ½ cup water in a large heavy-bottomed saucepan. Bring to a boil over high heat, swirling the pan occasionally, until all of the sugar is dissolved. Do not stir at this point. Wait until the sugar mixture turns to a medium amber color. Remove the pan from the heat and stir in the salt and butter. Pour the goat's milk in very slowly and stir with a wooden spoon. Continue stirring until the cajeta is smooth. Let cool before serving.

8

A MIDSUMMER NIGHT'S DINNER

There comes a point in the middle of summer when we barely want to eat hot food, and we certainly don't want to spend a lot of time cooking. Three of the four courses in this easy-to-prepare feast are served cold. Unlike a character out of Shakespeare, you won't have to wander "Over hill, over dale, through bush, through briar" to collect your ingredients. One trip to the farmers' market and a quick stop at the fishmonger—and don't forget the wine shop—and you can head straight to the beach, where the only work you will have to do is on your tan! Oh, and building a sand castle doesn't sound like a bad idea either.

APERITIVO:
Croft Pink Port and Soda

PORT GRAPE BLEND; PORTO, PORTUGAL

Gently pink and slightly sweet, this Port wine is not meant to be sipped in front of a roaring fireplace. It's a modern Port specifically designed to be mixed into cocktails. For an easy before-dinner drink, mix 1 to 2 ounces Croft Pink with 4 to 6 ounces club soda. Serve in a tall glass over ice.

APERITIVO: *Croft Pink and Soda*

COLD RED PEPPER SOUP WITH SPICY PEPPER-VODKA WHIPPED CREAM

WINE: *Mar de Frades Albariño*

STACKED TOMATO AND MOZZARELLA CAPRESE SALAD

WINE: *Bigi Est! Est! Est! de Montefiascone*

GRILLED SALT AND PEPPER TUNA OVER ZUCCHINI IN LEMON CAPER BUTTER

WINE: *Sartori di Verona Ferdi or Principessa Gavia*

BLOOD ORANGE-GRAPPA GRANITA

DIGESTIVO: *Alexander Grappa*

COLD RED PEPPER SOUP WITH SPICY PEPPER-VODKA WHIPPED CREAM

MAKES 8 SERVINGS

This refreshing take on gazpacho is an elegant start to your meal. The cold soup can be made a day or two in advance and refrigerated, so you can maximize your beach time. The whipped cream can be made at the last minute, as your housemates are gussying up for dinner. (Or better yet, when one of them asks, "Is there anything I can do?" just take the chilled mixing bowl out of the freezer and answer, "Why, yes, there is.")

Soup

2 to 3 tablespoons olive oil

I medium red onion, diced

½ teaspoon salt, plus more to taste

¼ teaspoon ground black pepper

I teaspoon Tabasco sauce

2 medium to large red bell peppers, cut into ¼-inch-wide strips

4 cups chicken stock, warm or at room temperature

2 teaspoons paprika

¼ teaspoon cayenne pepper

Whipped cream

½ cup heavy cream

2 tablespoons Stoli Pepper Vodka

¼ teaspoon fine salt

Paprika, for garnish

1. To make the soup: Heat 2 tablespoons oil in a large saucepan over medium heat. Add the onion, ½ teaspoon salt, and the black pepper, and stir frequently until the onion starts to wilt, about 3 minutes. Reduce the heat slightly and stir in the Tabasco. Add another 1 tablespoon oil if the pan seems dry. Add the bell peppers and stir until they soften, about 3 minutes. Add the chicken stock, bring to a boil, then reduce to a simmer, cover, and cook for 20 minutes. Stir in the paprika and cayenne and simmer for 10 minutes.

2. Set the saucepan aside to cool, uncovered, for 30 minutes. In two to three batches, transfer to a blender or food processor and process until smooth. Pour through a sieve into a glass bowl, stir, taste, and add more salt if necessary. Cover the bowl and refrigerate until ready to serve. (May be made 1 to 2 days ahead of time.)

3. To make the whipped cream: Chill the metal bowl of a stand or hand mixer in the freezer for at least 1 hour.

4. Pour the cream into the chilled bowl and whip at low to medium speed for a stand mixer, or high for a hand mixer, until the cream thickens and becomes foamy. Add the vodka and continue to whip until soft peaks form. Sprinkle the salt over the surface, and continue to whip for 30 seconds to mix in. Cover and refrigerate until ready to use.

5. To serve, for every portion, pour or ladle about 3 ounces (6 tablespoons) of soup into a 4- to 5-ounce liqueur glass. Using a teaspoon, float 2 to 3 teaspoons of spicy vodka whipped cream on the surface of each glass. If you're feeling extremely ambitious, use a pastry bag to pipe the whipped cream onto each serving. Dust the whipped cream with a touch of ground paprika. Serve with a teaspoon or long-handled iced tea spoon.

STACKED TOMATO AND MOZZARELLA CAPRESE SALAD

MAKES 8 SERVINGS

There are few starters that are as dramatic *and* so easy to make. Using perfectly ripe tomatoes and freshly made mozzarella, you can create a delicious architectural delight. Although this is a signature dish from the island of Capri, we first had this layered presentation in Porto Palo on the island of Sicily. Fresh basil, peppery olive oil, and sea salt bring out the earthy quality of the delicious tomatoes that grow in the island's mineral-rich volcanic soil.

8 medium tomatoes

2 balls (1 pound each) fresh mozzarella cheese

Coarse sea salt

64 basil leaves, well washed

¼ cup extra virgin olive oil

WINE:
Bigi Est! Est! Est! de Montefiascone

TREBBIANO AND MALVASIA; MONTEFIASCONE, LAZIO, ITALY

Forget "To be or not to be." Want to know if this fruity and floral white is a good wine?

Est! Est! Est! is Latin for "It is! It is! It is!"

1. Cut the stem end off each tomato so that it can stand upright on the plate and discard. Cut each tomato horizontally into 4 slices. Keep each tomato together and set aside. Horizontally cut each fresh mozzarella ball into 12 equal slices, for a total of 24.

2. To assemble, place the bottom slice of a tomato in the center of a salad plate. Salt lightly. Top with a slice of mozzarella and 2 basil leaves. Add another slice of tomato and repeat until each stacked salad is complete. Carefully spear each with a bamboo skewer to hold the layers together. Garnish with the remaining basil leaves. Do not refrigerate if you plan on serving in the next 90 minutes. When ready to serve, drizzle each stack with olive oil and sprinkle with a bit of sea salt.

GRILLED SALT AND PEPPER TUNA OVER ZUCCHINI IN LEMON CAPER BUTTER

MAKES 8 SERVINGS

Many of our friends who no longer eat red meat say they enjoy tuna because it has the weight and feel of a good steak. This effortless preparation is the fish-lover's version of steak au poivre. The zucchini with lemon caper butter adds a bright note to your dinner plate.

Tuna

3 pounds sushi-grade tuna

½ cup coarsely ground black pepper

¼ cup coarse sea salt

Zucchini

8 zucchini

¼ cup extra virgin olive oil

Coarse salt

Coarsely ground black pepper

Lemon caper butter

8 tablespoons (1 stick) salted butter

2 tablespoons capers

Juice of 2 lemons

½ teaspoon salt

½ teaspoon ground black pepper

1. To prepare the tuna: Slice the tuna into 8 equal steaks. Combine the pepper and salt in a small bowl and pour onto a clean dinner plate. Press each tuna steak into the mixture to coat evenly. Refrigerate until ready to grill.

2. To prepare the zucchini: Preheat the grill to medium. Cut each zucchini lengthwise into 5 or 6 strips. Lay flat, brush with oil, and sprinkle with salt and pepper. Grill for 1 for 2 minutes per side, until lightly browned. Set aside.

3. To make the lemon caper butter: Melt the butter in a small saucepan. Add the capers and cook for 2 minutes. Add the lemon juice, salt, and pepper and cook for 2 minutes to heat through.

4. Add the tuna steaks to the grill and grill for 2 to 3 minutes on each side for medium-rare.

5. To assemble, place 5 or 6 zucchini strips in the center of each plate. Drizzle with lemon caper butter. Top each plate of zucchini with a tuna steak.

WINE:

Sartori di Verona Ferdi

GARGANEGA; VERONA,
VENETO, ITALY

Like Shakespeare's two
gentlemen, this pear- and apricot-
flavored white hails from Verona.

OR

Principessa Gavia, Gavi

CORTESE; GAVI,
PIEDMONT, ITALY

This wine comes with its own
Romeo and Juliet story, which
you can read on the label. Unlike
the Bard's version, this crisp
white has a pleasant finish.

BLOOD ORANGE- GRAPPA GRANITA

MAKES 8 SERVINGS

Italians love their delicious blood oranges and for good reason. Although blood orange season in the States is winter, these fruits are grown around the world and can usually be found in high-end markets in the summer.

15 to 18 blood oranges *or* 4 cups blood orange juice

⅔ cup superfine or bar sugar

3 tablespoons grappa

DIGESTIVO:
Alexander Grappa

VENICE, VENETO, ITALY

It takes only one merchant of Venice, Sandro Bottega, to distill this refined digestif *and* design the beautiful handblown Murano glass bottle it comes in.

1. If using oranges, squeeze them into a strainer set over a large measuring cup. (Or use a manual or electric juicer.) Pour the juice into a large glass bowl. Stir in the sugar until dissolved and transfer to a 13 by 9-inch glass baking dish.

2. Place the dish in the freezer for 1 hour, until the juice and sugar mixture begins to get slushy. Stir in the grappa, blending well. Cover the dish with plastic wrap and return to the freezer for at least 4 hours, until frozen. (You may make this up to 1 day in advance.)

3. To serve, scrape the surface of the ice with a heavy metal fork, to create small shavings. Working quickly, transfer to small bowls or coffee cups, and serve immediately.

9

PAELLA BEACH PARTY

The best paella in Spain is always found at beachfront restaurants, where it is generally eaten at lunchtime. A few years ago, it was hard to find good paella pans in the States, but with the rise in popularity of Spanish food, you can find them anywhere that pots and pans are sold. The best part of any paella is the *socarrat*— the crust that forms on the bottom of the pan, adding an extra special crunch to the saffron-scented rice. Make sure to choose a nice wide-bottomed pan, because the more surface area you have, the more of this delectable treat you and your friends will get to enjoy. In Spain, only tourists eat paella at dinnertime. But hey, you're on vacation; it's okay to act like a tourist every once in a while.

APERITIVO:
Juvé y Camps Brut Rosé

PINOT NOIR; CAVA, PENEDÈS, SPAIN

No Spaniard would think about starting a party without a glass of Cava. Made from 100 percent Pinot Noir, the vibrant flavors and aromas only hint at the exciting dinner to come.

APERITIVO: *Juvé y Camps Brut Rosé*

TAPAS BAR SEAFOOD SALAD
WINE: *Laxas Albariño*

PAELLA WITH SHELLFISH AND CHORIZO
WINE: *Dominio de Tares Godello*

GRILLED ENDIVE IN ROMESCO SAUCE
WINE: *Vivanco Blanco*

TOCINO DE CIELO WITH ORANGE-SCENTED WHIPPED CREAM
WINE: *Domecq Venerable Pedro Ximénez Sherry*

TAPAS BAR SEAFOOD SALAD

MAKES 8 SERVINGS

When you walk into a bar in Spain, you will see a glass-covered case filled with salads and cooked foods. With each glass of wine you order, you will be offered a *tapa*, or small plate of food—for free! Cold seafood salad is always a sure bet, especially with a nice, crisp glass of Albariño.

1 pound octopus

1½ pounds medium shrimp

¾ pound cooked crabmeat, fresh or canned

1 small red bell pepper, cut into ¼-inch-wide strips

1 small green bell pepper, cut into ¼-inch-wide strips

1 medium red onion, diced

½ pound green olives, pitted

½ cup extra virgin olive oil

¼ cup fresh lemon juice

Salt and ground black pepper

WINE:
Laxas Albariño

ABARIÑO; RIAS BAIXAS, GALICIA, SPAIN

The bracing minerality of this clean white wine is just right with seafood.

1. In a large pan of boiling salted water, cook the octopus until tender, 30 minutes to 1 hour, depending on the thickness of the octopus. When cool enough to handle, cut into ¼-inch slices.

2. Peel the shrimp and remove the tails. In a medium saucepan, bring salted water to a boil over high heat. Add the shrimp and cook until they turn pink, 3 to 5 minutes. Drain and rinse under cold running water.

3. Break the crabmeat into ½-inch pieces with your fingers and a fork. Place the shrimp, octopus, and crabmeat in a large glass or ceramic bowl. Add the bell peppers, onion, and olives and toss lightly. Add the oil and lemon juice, and mix to coat the seafood and vegetables. Season lightly with salt and black pepper to taste. Refrigerate and serve cold. (This can be made in the morning and plated at dinnertime.)

PAELLA WITH SHELLFISH AND CHORIZO

MAKES 8 SERVINGS

Although Americans tend to think of paella as being made only with shellfish, any rice dish prepared in this manner bears the name. We have seen versions made with chicken, pork, *morcilla* (blood sausage), and even rabbit. One of the restaurants on the beach near our house in Spain is famous for its delicious seafood paella made in a giant pan the size of a child's swimming pool. This is our take on the classic version.

10 to 12 cups chicken stock

1 packet Goya Sazón con Azafrán (seasoning with saffron)

½ cup olive oil

2 large onions, diced

Salt and ground black pepper

2 teaspoons Tabasco or hot sauce

½ pound chorizo, finely diced

2 pounds arborio rice

1 medium to large red bell pepper, finely diced

1 cup frozen peas

8 to 12 mussels (see Tip)

8 to 12 clams (see Tip)

8 large peeled and deveined shrimp

1. Heat 2 cups of the stock in the microwave in a glass measuring cup and stir in the Goya Sazón.

2. Preheat a large, high-sided skillet over medium heat. Add the oil and heat until it sizzles. Add the onions, season lightly with salt and black pepper, and cook until soft and golden. Stir in the Tabasco and cook, stirring frequently so the onions don't burn. Stir in the chorizo, and when the chorizo is softened and starts to color the onions, stir the rice into the pan.

3. Add the stock (including the seasoned stock) to the rice in ½-cup increments, stirring until each pouring of liquid is absorbed, and then add more. (It is hard to know exactly how much liquid you will use; depending on heat and time, it will be between 10 and 12 cups.) After about 15 minutes of stirring in liquid, add the bell pepper and peas to the rice. The total stirring time for the rice is 20 to 25 minutes. Stir frequently so that the rice does not stick.

(continued)

WINE:

*Dominio de Tares
Godello*

GODELLO; BIERZO, SPAIN

Lemon and apple notes with a
creamy mouthfeel pair nicely with
the rich rice, spice, and shellfish.

4. Preheat the oven to 350°F.

5. Transfer the rice to one large or two smaller shallow, two-handled pans. Nestle the mussels, clams, and shrimp into the top of the rice. Bake until the mussels and clams open and the shrimp are pink, 10 to 15 minutes. Serve immediately.

TIP: This dish looks best and makes the most sense with 1 mussel, 1 clam, and 1 shrimp per person, but since we sometimes find ourselves with one or two mollusks that don't open, it might be best to have a few extra—maybe a dozen of each—to make sure everybody gets one. To clean the mussels and clams, place them in a bowl in a sink and run cold water into the bowl. Let sit for a few minutes, dump out the water, and repeat. Do this several times, until you are no longer getting sand in the bottom of the bowl with each rinse.

GRILLED ENDIVE IN ROMESCO SAUCE

MAKES 8 SERVINGS

Romesco is a type of sauce from the north of Spain made with peppers and bread. It is often served over grilled vegetables, but the sauce is also terrific with chicken or pork. This grilled salad is a nice segue into dessert.

Romesco sauce

3 tablespoons olive oil, for frying

I red bell pepper, cut into thin strips

I clove garlic, peeled but whole

2 small tomatoes, seeded and chopped

½ teaspoon salt

¼ teaspoon cayenne pepper

¼ teaspoon red pepper flakes

⅓ cup slivered almonds

½ cup leftover Italian or French bread, torn into small cubes

½ cup extra virgin olive oil

Endive

¼ to ½ cup olive oil

I to 2 tablespoons coarse salt

8 small to medium endives

1. To make the romesco sauce: Heat 2 tablespoons of the olive oil in a medium saucepan over medium heat. Add the bell pepper and garlic and cook, stirring, until soft. Add the tomatoes, salt, cayenne, and red pepper flakes, and cook, stirring, for 2 minutes. Move the ingredients to the side of the pan, add the remaining 1 tablespoon olive oil to the center, then add the almonds and bread, stirring until coated. Remove from the heat and transfer to a large food processor. Begin to pulse, gradually adding small amounts of the ½ cup olive oil until the sauce reaches a smooth consistency. Due to varying water content of peppers and tomatoes, you may not need to use all the olive oil. (The sauce can be made a day or two ahead of time and refrigerated. Bring back to room temperature for serving.)

2. To prepare the endive: Preheat the grill to medium.

(continued)

3. Pour a few tablespoons of the oil into the bottom of a 1-gallon resealable plastic bag, and add about 1 tablespoon of coarse salt. Place 2 to 3 endives at a time in the bag and shake until coated. Set aside on a plate and repeat until all 8 of the endives are done, adding small amounts of olive oil and salt with each batch, if necessary.

4. Grill the endives for 5 to 7 minutes, turning once, until lightly browned and beginning to wilt.

5. To serve, place an endive in the center of a salad plate and spoon 2 to 3 tablespoons of room-temperature romesco sauce over each one. Serve immediately.

WELCOME TO FIRE ISLAND PI
A FAMILY COMMUNITY

We Believe In a Community that is clean both mor and physically.

We Believe That riotous parties disturb the peace and of our community.

We Believe The bikini type bathing apparel tends to lo the moral standards of a community.

We Believe That exhibitionism in public is below the level human behavior

We Believe That everyone living at the PINES wants to uphold the commo standards of decency relating to personal conduct.

These beliefs are being publicized in the interest of the many CHILDREN in our community who we feel should have the opportunity of growing up in healthy surroundings. THIS IS THE HOPE OF THE FUTURE, and THE COVENANT OF EVERY ADULT!

The Fire Island Pines Property Owners Assn.

Original
PINES
SIGN
Circa 1957

TOCINO DE CIELO WITH ORANGE-SCENTED WHIPPED CREAM

MAKES 8 SERVINGS

There is no clear consensus as to how this decadent egg custard got its name, which means "bacon from heaven." In Spain, these and other egg yolk–based sweets are traditionally made by nuns: the egg whites are used in the winemaking process (for filtering out solids) and the yolks were donated to the nuns, who baked desserts with them and sold them to make money for charitable causes. In fact, at church gift shops in many small Spanish towns, you can still buy this and other delights made by nuns. So whether the "heaven" in the name has to do with the nuns, or with where you will think you have died and gone to after just one bite, we are sure you will love this simple treat.

12 egg yolks

2 cups granulated sugar

1 cup heavy cream

¼ cup confectioners' sugar

2 tablespoons Cointreau (orange liqueur)

WINE:
Domecq Venerable Pedro Ximénez Sherry

PEDRO XIMÉNEZ; JEREZ, SPAIN

A bold, deep-red dessert sherry tasting of stewed fruits and molasses with a touch of vanilla.

1. Preheat the oven to 350°F. Place the egg yolks in a glass bowl.

2. Combine the granulated sugar with 1 cup water in a small saucepan. Heat over medium to high heat, stirring frequently with a wooden spoon. When the mixture comes to a boil, reduce the heat slightly and continue to stir until the sugar starts to brown, about 5 minutes. Pour a small amount of the syrup into an 8 by 8-inch glass baking dish, shaking the dish lightly to coat the bottom. Set the remaining sugar syrup aside to cool slightly.

3. Whisk the egg yolks until smooth, then whisk in small amounts of the warm sugar syrup, stirring constantly so the eggs do not begin to cook. When all the sugar syrup is incorporated into the egg yolks, pour the mixture into the baking dish.

4. Set the baking dish into a larger pan and pour water into the larger pan to a depth of 1 inch. Place in the oven and bake until the eggs have set and a wooden pick inserted into the center comes out clean, 1½ to 2 hours. The syrup will rise to the top, creating a meringue-like crust. Let cool.

5. Meanwhile, to make the whipped cream: Chill the metal bowl of a stand or hand mixer in the freezer for at least 1 hour. Pour the cream into the chilled bowl, add the confectioners' sugar, and whip at low to medium speed for a stand mixer, or high for a hand mixer, until the cream thickens and becomes foamy. Add the Cointreau and continue to whip until soft peaks form. Cover and refrigerate until ready to use.

6. To serve, run a thin metal spatula around the edges of the baking dish to loosen the custard. Cut into 8 equal portions and carefully remove with a small, flexible spatula. Turn each piece over onto a small plate, so that the crust is on the bottom and the shiny custard faces up. Serve each square with a dollop of orange-scented whipped cream.

TIP: Whipped cream is best when freshly made. If you want to make it ahead of time, do so just before your guests arrive—the longer it sits, the more volume and airiness it loses.

10
MEDITERRANEAN ODYSSEY

Food from the Mediterranean makes perfect sense at the shore. After all, countries that border this placid body of water experience some of the best beach weather anywhere in the world, and the slowed-down pace of life is ideal for days filled with sun and sand. This dinner takes a hop, skip, and a jump around the whole region, with flavors—and wines to match—from Italy, Spain, France, and Greece. In the meantime, the Fire Island waves are calling, so take a hop, skip, and a jump of your own to the vegetable market, the butcher, and the baker, and then get back outside and enjoy the day.

TRIO OF ARUGULA PESTO, RED PEPPER, AND BLACK OLIVE BRUSCHETTA
WINE: *Planeta La Segreta Bianco*

HARICOTS VERTS WITH GRAPE TOMATOES AND ALMONDS
WINE: *Palacios Remondo Plácet*

HERBES DE PROVENCE GRILLED LAMB CHOPS WITH BLEU D'AUVERGNE MASHED POTATOES
WINE: *Père Anselme La Fiole du Pape Châteauneuf-du-Pape or Domaine Grosset Côtes du Rhône Villages Cairanne*

GREEK YOGURT WITH HOMEMADE FIG COMPOTE
WINE: *Gai'a Anatolikos*

TRIO OF ARUGULA PESTO, RED PEPPER, AND BLACK OLIVE BRUSCHETTA

MAKES 8 SERVINGS

In Italy, *bruschetta* refers to grilled bread with toppings, often consisting of garlic, tomato, and extra virgin olive oil. In the States, the word has come to mean any type of vaguely Italian topping to be spread on bread, usually as an appetizer. This trio of toppings, as delicious as it is attractive, is a virtual trip around the Mediterranean: we went to Italy for the arugula pesto, to Spain for the red pepper, and to France for the niçoise olives, but we brought it all back to our friends on Fire Island.

The technique is the same for all three of these savory spreads, but note the differing amounts of olive oil. The variation is due to the inconsistent water quantity in the main flavor components: arugula, red pepper, and olives. Remember to drizzle the oil slowly through the small hole in your food processor's feed tube, stopping when you have reached the proper consistency. Ideally, the toppings should be able to hold their shape on a plate but should spread easily on bread, similar to cream cheese or room-temperature butter. You can make all three of these, start to finish, in under an hour, and you don't even need to clean the food processor in between batches if you scrape all your spreads out well enough. Trust us, you won't want to waste a single teaspoonful! These may be made 2 to 3 days ahead of time, and they're great to have on hand in case friends drop by on their way home from the beach.

WINE:
Planeta La Segreta Bianco

GREGANICO-CHARDONNAY
BLEND; SICILY, ITALY

From the heart of the Mediterranean, this enjoyable white evokes the flavors of clementines and honeydew melon.

(continued)

117

Arugula pesto topping

1 can (15.5 ounces) chickpeas, drained

¼ pound Parmesan cheese, cut into small cubes

2 cups tightly packed arugula leaves

1 tablespoon fresh lemon juice

½ teaspoon salt

½ teaspoon ground black pepper

⅓ cup olive oil

Red pepper topping

¾ pound red bell peppers (2 to 3 small to medium)

Olive oil

Salt

1 can (15.5 ounces) chickpeas, drained

¼ pound Parmesan cheese, cut into small cubes

½ teaspoon red wine vinegar

½ teaspoon ground black pepper

¼ teaspoon cayenne pepper

3 tablespoons extra virgin olive oil

1. To make the arugula pesto topping: Combine the chickpeas, Parmesan, arugula, lemon juice, salt, and pepper in a food processor and process until a thick paste is formed. Scrape down the sides, then, with the machine running, slowly drizzle in the oil through the processor's feed tube until a spreadable consistency is reached. Transfer to an airtight plastic container and refrigerate.

2. To make the red pepper topping: Preheat the oven to 350°F. Brush the bell peppers with some oil and salt lightly. Roast for 30 minutes. Remove from the oven, place in a glass bowl, and cover the bowl with plastic wrap. Let sit for 15 minutes, until the peppers "wilt" and lose much of their liquid. Transfer to a cutting board and remove the skin, stem, ribs, and seeds. Drain off any excess liquid, pat the peppers dry with paper towels, and transfer to a food processor.

3. Add the chickpeas, Parmesan, vinegar, ½ teaspoon salt, the black pepper, and cayenne to the processor and process until a thick paste is formed. Scrape down the sides, then, with the machine running, slowly drizzle in the extra virgin olive oil through the processor's feed tube until a spreadable consistency is reached. Transfer to an airtight plastic container and refrigerate.

Black olive topping

1 can (15.5 ounces) chickpeas, drained

¼ pound Parmesan cheese, cut into small cubes

1 cup pitted niçoise olives (see Tip)

½ teaspoon ground black pepper

¼ cup extra virgin olive oil

Bruschetta

2 French baguettes, thinly sliced

4. To make the black olive topping: Combine the chickpeas, Parmesan, olives, and pepper in a food processor and process until a thick paste is formed. Scrape down the sides, then, with the machine running, slowly drizzle the oil through the processor's feed tube until a spreadable consistency is reached. (You may not use all of the oil, depending on the water content in the olives.) Transfer to an airtight plastic container and refrigerate.

5. To assemble the bruschetta: Using a small ice-cream scoop or a soup spoon, arrange a small mound of each topping on each of 8 plates. Place 6 to 8 slices of baguette on each plate and serve.

TIP: If you use oil-cured olives instead—the kind with a wrinkled appearance, like large raisins—you will need to increase the amount of olive oil by several tablespoons.

HARICOTS VERTS WITH GRAPE TOMATOES AND ALMONDS

MAKES 8 SERVINGS

This appetizer is bright on both the plate and the palate, and it is also a Mediterranean hybrid: the haricots verts are distinctly French, but the almonds and sherry vinegar lend a taste of Spain to the dish.

1½ pounds haricots verts or thin green beans

2 pints small grape tomatoes, halved (or quartered if you can't find small ones)

¼ cup extra virgin olive oil

3 tablespoons sherry vinegar

½ teaspoon salt

¼ teaspoon ground black pepper

⅓ cup slivered almonds

WINE:
Palacios Remondo Plácet

VIURA; RIOJA, SPAIN

The refreshing fruit and almond notes of this northern Spanish white are a strong match to the vibrant flavors of this dish.

1. Bring a large saucepan half filled with salted water to a rolling boil, add the beans, and blanch for 3 minutes. Drain in a colander and spray with cold running water. Cover the beans with a cup of ice cubes and let drain in the sink. (The cold running water and ice will stop the beans from cooking, and they will retain their bright green color.)

2. Toss together the beans and tomatoes in a large glass bowl. Whisk together the oil and vinegar and pour over the beans and tomatoes. Sprinkle with the salt and pepper, and toss until the beans are coated with dressing and tomato water. Using tongs or a slotted spoon, transfer to 8 salad plates, evenly distributing any dressing remaining in the bottom of the bowl. Sprinkle the almonds over each portion and serve. (This may be made several hours ahead of time and stored in the refrigerator, uncovered. Do not add the almonds until ready to serve.)

HERBES DE PROVENCE GRILLED LAMB CHOPS WITH BLEU D'AUVERGNE MASHED POTATOES

MAKES 8 SERVINGS

The first time we cycled through Provençal fields of rosemary, lavender, thyme, and oregano, we totally understood the culinary concept of herbes de Provence.

16 single-cut rib lamb chops, 2½ to 3 pounds (see Tip)

¼ cup herbes de Provence

1 tablespoon fine sea salt

1 tablespoon finely ground white pepper

Bleu d'Auvergne Mashed Potatoes (page 124)

Rosemary, oregano, or thyme sprigs, for garnish

WINE:
Père Anselme La Fiole du Pape Châteauneuf-du-Pape

GRENACHE BLEND; RHÔNE VALLEY, FRANCE

Earthy aromas of truffles, dark fruits, and spiced wood give way to a luxurious finish.

OR

Domaine Grosset Côtes du Rhône Villages Cairanne

GRENACHE BLEND; RHÔNE VALLEY, FRANCE

Up-front notes of blackberry and wild cherry yield to black pepper and lightly buttered toast.

1. Preheat the grill to medium.

2. Sprinkle the lamb chops evenly on both sides with the herbes de Provence, salt, and pepper. Grill the chops for 3 to 3½ minutes per side for medium-rare.

3. To serve, place a 3½-inch biscuit cutter or pastry ring in the center of a plate. Fill with the blue cheese mashed potatoes, patting down firmly. Remove the ring and arrange 2 lamb chops on each plate. Garnish with rosemary, oregano, or thyme sprigs.

TIP: Ask the butcher for 16 equal rib chops. If you want a more elegant look, ask him to "french" the rib bones, which means he will remove the extra fat and meat from the bone. Remember to cover the exposed ends of the bones with foil before grilling to prevent the bones from burning. Remove the foil before serving.

BLEU D'AUVERGNE MASHED POTATOES

MAKES 8 SERVINGS

One of our Fire Island friends always says, "If you take something good and add something good . . . it's gotta be good." Over the years, it has become one of our private jokes when we make these delicious blue cheese mashed potatoes.

12 medium red potatoes, cut into 1-inch cubes

1½ teaspoons salt

½ cup whole milk

4 tablespoons salted butter

1 teaspoon ground white pepper

½ pound bleu d'Auvergne cheese

1. Combine the potatoes, cold water to cover, and 1 teaspoon of the salt in a saucepan. Bring to a boil over high heat and cook until the potato chunks can be mashed with a fork, 10 to 12 minutes after the boiling begins. Drain the potatoes, rinse once with cold water, and return to the pot.

2. Combine the milk and butter in a glass measuring cup and microwave for 45 seconds. Slowly add the hot milk to the potatoes as you hand-mash them. Add the remaining ½ teaspoon salt, the pepper, and blue cheese and combine well.

GREEK YOGURT WITH HOMEMADE FIG COMPOTE

MAKES 8 SERVINGS

Yogurt is amazingly refreshing and soothing after a heavy meal. We suggest using a good-quality store-bought Greek yogurt. Traditionally the Greeks eat plain, unflavored yogurt, but you can substitute vanilla if you prefer. The homemade fig compote uses fresh figs and takes a bit of time—but your guests will be able to taste the difference.

1½ pounds fresh figs

1½ cups sugar

Grated zest of 1 lemon

3 cups Greek yogurt

WINE:
Gai'a Anatolikos

AGIORGITIKO;
NEMEA, GREECE

This sweet wine made from sun-dried Agiorgitiko grapes has flavors of strawberry marmalade and honey.

1. Cut the stems off the figs and place the figs in a medium saucepan. Add the sugar, lemon zest, and ½ cup water. Cook, uncovered, over medium heat until the figs have broken down and the liquid resembles a thick syrup, about 1 hour, stirring frequently to avoid burning. Let cool for 20 minutes. Transfer to a glass bowl and refrigerate for at least 3 hours or, better yet, overnight.

2. To serve, divide the yogurt among 8 small glass bowls. Spoon 2 to 3 teaspoons of fig compote on top of the yogurt.

11

AMERICA
THE BOUNTIFUL

In addition to all the travel we have undertaken to Europe and the Southern Hemisphere for our wine writing, we have also been lucky enough to visit some wonderful wine regions right here at home. Although most Americans think only about the West Coast—California, Oregon, and Washington—when considering wine, we have also found excellent examples in Virginia and in New York—on Long Island and in the Hudson Valley. Believe it or not, grapes are grown and wine is made in all fifty states. If, like us, you try to eat seasonal, local foods as much as possible, it is definitely a good idea to try some local wines and make them part of your own personal farm-to-table movement.

There is truly nothing more wonderful than buying vegetables at local farmers' markets, and as lovers of all things pork, we are especially excited when we come across a cooler in New York City's Union Square filled with chops and fresh-cured bacon. We are so blessed to live a short drive from the Hudson Valley,

HAND-SHUCKED CORN AND TOMATO SALAD
WINE: *Hearst Ranch Three Sisters Cuvée White*

GRILLED ROMAINE BLT SALAD
WINE: *Boxwood Rosé*

PEPPERCORN BRINED PORK CHOPS WITH GRILLED SWEET PEACHES
WINE: *Hudson-Chatham Cabernet Franc or Heron Pinot Noir*

SALTED CHOCOLATE CARAMEL BROWNIES
PAIRING: *Buffalo Trace Kentucky Straight Bourbon Whiskey*

and we know that all across this wonderful country there are small family farmers turning their backs on the industrial practices that produce most of the food we would otherwise have to eat. So when it comes time to cook up that all-American meal, even though it costs a little more and may even be out of the way, remember it's always a good idea to "Think global, act local."

HAND-SHUCKED CORN AND TOMATO SALAD

MAKES 8 SERVINGS

Locally grown corn and tomatoes are plentiful on Long Island from July through September. There are so many ways to use them at mealtime, and one of our favorites is this simple salad—the fresh flavors really speak of summer. The minerality and bright acidity of the tomato combine beautifully with the delicate creaminess of the sweet corn. We always use a superior-quality cold-pressed extra virgin olive oil. There are some excellent oils coming from California wine country. The subtle yet luscious peppered flavor is the perfect complement to this salad.

4 ears freshly picked local white corn

4 ears freshly picked local yellow corn

8 large locally grown tomatoes, ripe and juicy

1 teaspoon salt

1 teaspoon coarsely ground black pepper

½ cup extra virgin olive oil

WINE:
Hearst Ranch Three Sisters Cuvée White

GRENACHE BLANC-MARSANNE BLEND; PASO ROBLES, CALIFORNIA.

Hints of tangerine, orange blossom, and apricot along with racy brightness make this a wine you'll want to start every meal with.

1. Shuck the corn, making sure to remove all of the silk threads. Stand each ear on end and use a sharp knife to cut the kernels off the cob. Core and seed the tomatoes. Cut the tomatoes into 8 wedges and then cut each wedge into 2 or 3 pieces.

2. Toss the corn and tomatoes together in a large glass bowl and season with the salt and pepper. Add the oil and toss. Cover with plastic wrap and let sit for 1 to 2 hours before serving. This allows all of the flavors to meld together.

GRILLED ROMAINE BLT SALAD

MAKES 8 SERVINGS

A BLT sandwich is a childhood favorite of both of us. This grilled romaine salad gives you all of the flavor without carb-heavy bread.

¾ cup extra virgin olive oil, plus extra for grilling the lettuce

½ pound blue cheese, crumbled

1 tablespoon white wine vinegar

1 teaspoon salt

1 teaspoon ground black pepper

½ pound thick-cut maple-smoked bacon

4 small heads romaine lettuce

4 medium locally grown tomatoes, sliced

WINE:
Boxwood Rosé

CABERNET SAUVIGNON AND MERLOT;
MIDDLEBURG, VIRGINIA

This easy-to-quaff American pink is like strawberries and cream in a bottle.

1. Whisk together the ¾ cup oil, the cheese, vinegar, salt, and pepper in a glass bowl.

2. Place the bacon in a cold cast-iron skillet and turn the heat to medium-high. Cook the bacon until crispy. Drain on a paper towel.

3. Preheat the grill to medium. Remove the outer leaves from the romaine and discard. Halve the heads lengthwise. Brush with some extra virgin olive oil and grill for 2 minutes per side, until the romaine is wilted and has grill marks.

4. To serve, place one romaine half on each plate. Drizzle with a small amount of the salad dressing. Arrange 3 tomato slices over the lettuce. Crumble the bacon over each and dress with the remaining dressing. Serve while the lettuce is warm.

PEPPERCORN BRINED PORK CHOPS

MAKES 8 SERVINGS

Who doesn't love a big juicy grilled pork chop? This recipe is so simple and takes only minutes in the kitchen. We like to brine our pork chops for 24 hours, so we make the brine a day ahead of time. We are enamored of European pork, which tends to have a higher fat content than its American counterpart, but the brine adds moisture that your pork might otherwise lack. If you can get locally raised, free-range pork from a farm stand or butcher, you will be rewarded with some of the most succulent pig you have ever sunk your teeth into.

½ cup coarse salt

½ cup sugar

¼ cup whole black peppercorns

I dried habanero pepper

8 boneless thick-cut (1 ½ inches) pork chops (see Tip)

Thyme sprigs, for garnish

1. Bring 4 quarts of water to a rolling boil. Add the salt, sugar, peppercorns, and habanero. Cover and boil for 10 minutes. Remove from the heat and let cool to room temperature.

2. When the brine is cool, place the pork chops in the brine. Make sure that they are completely submerged. Cover and refrigerate overnight.

3. When you're ready to cook the pork chops, preheat the grill for at least 10 minutes so it will be hot enough to sear the meat. Pat the pork chops dry with paper towels and grill them for 4 to 5 minutes on each side, until a meat thermometer reads 150°F. Let rest for 3 minutes before serving with Grilled Sweet Peaches (recipe follows) and enjoy!

TIP: We usually use boneless pork chops for even cooking times. In our childhood, everyone, including our mothers, teachers, and the media, warned against eating undercooked pork. The beauty about brining pork chops is that the salt kills most of the bacteria so you don't have to overcook the meat until it is dry and inedible. Brined meats remain moist, juicy, and, most of all, delicious.

GRILLED SWEET PEACHES

MAKES 8 SERVINGS

Both white and yellow varieties work well for this simple side dish. Choose slightly harder, firmer peaches—they'll grill better.

6 locally grown peaches, quartered

3 tablespoons extra virgin olive oil

½ teaspoon salt

½ teaspoon finely ground white pepper

2 tablespoons balsamic vinegar

1. Preheat the grill to medium-high.

2. Brush the peaches all over with the oil and sprinkle with the salt and pepper. Grill, turning to get all sides, until lightly browned and softened, 5 to 7 minutes. Remove from the heat and transfer to a plate. Drizzle with the vinegar. Serve while warm.

SALTED CHOCOLATE CARAMEL BROWNIES

MAKES 8 SERVINGS

Chocolate, salt, and caramel represent three of our favorite food groups. Brownies are the quintessential American dessert, but our addition of salted caramel sauce comes from a taste sensation we discovered while driving around the western wine regions of France. Each time we stopped for gas, we would run into the truck-stop market to buy delicious chewy caramels made with the local sea salt, *fleur de sel,* from the Île de Ré. These brownies are a combination of the best gooey sweet desserts from two of our favorite countries.

Brownies

8 ounces unsweetened chocolate

½ pound (2 sticks) butter (see Tip)

2 cups sugar

3 eggs

I cup all-purpose flour

¼ teaspoon fine sea salt

Salted caramel sauce

I cup sugar

6 tablespoons butter

½ cup heavy cream

I teaspoon fine sea salt

I tablespoon fleur de sel

1. To make the brownies: Preheat the oven to 350°F. Butter a 9 by 12-inch metal baking pan.

2. Match a large saucepan with a metal bowl big enough to sit over, not in, the pan, to make a double boiler. Fill the pan halfway with water and bring it to a boil. Make sure the bottom of the bowl won't come in direct contact with the water. Place the chocolate and butter in the bowl and stir until melted. Whisk in the sugar. Remove from the heat and let rest.

3. Whisk the eggs in a separate bowl. Little by little, whisk the hot chocolate mixture into the eggs, whisking constantly, until completely mixed. Slowly add the flour and salt and stir until everything is well mixed. Pour the mixture into the baking pan and bake until a toothpick inserted into the center of the pan comes out relatively clean and the cake begins to pull away from the edges of the pan, about 25 minutes. Be careful not to overcook. Let the brownies cool in the pan on a rack for about 20 minutes.

(continued)

PAIRING:

Buffalo Trace Kentucky Straight Bourbon Whiskey

FRANKFORT, KENTUCKY

Vanilla, dark brown sugar, and leather notes in this formidable spirit will not be overpowered by these decadent brownies.

4. Meanwhile, to make the salted caramel sauce: Heat the sugar in a heavy-bottomed 3-quart saucepan over medium to high heat while whisking constantly. When the sugar begins bubbling, stop stirring and wait until the sugar begins to caramelize to an amber color. Add the butter and begin whisking again. After all of the butter is melted, remove the pan from the heat and add the heavy cream a little at a time. It is important to continue whisking at this stage. Don't worry: it's normal for the cream to foam up—just keep mixing. When all of the cream is added and the foaming stops, add the fine sea salt and stir well. Let the salted caramel sauce rest until the brownies come out of the oven.

5. While the brownies are still slightly warm (and in the pan), pour the caramel sauce over the top until evenly coated. (If the caramel sauce has begun to harden and becomes difficult to pour, just heat it up for a minute or two.) Sprinkle with fleur de sel and let cool for 2 hours. (The pan can be refrigerated for a few days if you want to make the brownies ahead of time; the hard part is keeping your housemates' fingers out of the pan.)

TIP: Save the butter wrappers to grease the baking pan.

12

VILLA IN TUSCANY

As much as we love the beach, every now and then we love to rent a house in the mountains and fill it up with friends. We did this a few years back in Tuscany, and although we enjoyed our dinners out, the most memorable nights were those on which we all went to the market together in the morning and then each lent a hand cooking dinner that same evening. For people who grew up shopping in grocery stores—where meat came in Styrofoam trays and tomatoes were packed in little plastic baskets—there is something exciting about going to three or four different shops and even an open-air market while traveling. What is even more thrilling today is that the pendulum has swung back in the other direction, and that anywhere in the United States we can find outdoor stalls selling heirloom vegetables on weekend mornings, and we can stop by the butcher and chat a little before holding our fingers a couple of inches apart to show him how thick we want the *bistecca*.

APERITIVO:
Ferrari Brut

SPARKLING 100 PERCENT
CHARDONNAY; TRENTINO, ITALY

Clean and balanced, this Italian sparkler is an ideal start to any Italian feast.

APERITIVO: *Ferrari Brut*

PENNE WITH PROSCIUTTO AND PEAS
WINE: *Cabreo La Pietra*

BISTECCA ALLA FIORENTINA
WINE: *Carpineto Chianti Classico Riserva or Feudi di San Gregorio Taurasi DOCG*

SHAVED FENNEL SALAD
WINE: *Poggio alle Gazze Toscana IGT Bianco*

CINNAMON CARAMELIZED GNOCCHI
WINE: *Rosa Regale*

PENNE WITH PROSCIUTTO AND PEAS

MAKES 8 SERVINGS

The Italian word for colander or strainer is *scolapasta,* which is a shortened version of "drain the pasta." In the Brooklyn Sicilian dialect of Mike's grandparents, this word is pronounced "school-a-bast." When our Sicilian friend Chiara Planeta heard us use this pronunciation of the word, the only thing she could say was, "Surely, this is a joke." The joke was really on us, as it was a revelation when we heard the real way that this useful word is spoken. In this recipe, you will use two "school-a-basts": a small one to thaw the peas, and a larger one for its intended use, draining the pasta.

2 cups frozen peas, thawed (or fresh shelled, if you can find them)

2 tablespoons salt

1½ pounds penne pasta

½ cup olive oil

¼ pound thinly sliced prosciutto, cut or torn into small pieces

¼ pound Locatelli Romano cheese, grated

Ground black pepper

WINE:
Cabreo La Pietra

CHARDONNAY; FLORENCE, TUSCANY, ITALY

Aged six months in French oak barrels, this 100 percent Italian Chardonnay has flavors of peach, butter, and vanilla.

1. Place the frozen peas in a small colander to thaw and come to room temperature. Place the colander in the sink or over a small plate to catch the dripping water. (If using fresh peas, cook them in boiling water for 2 minutes, drain, and allow to come to room temperature before using. With frozen, let them start thawing when you head to the beach in the morning.)

2. Fill a large, heavy-bottomed pot half to two-thirds with cold water, stir in the salt, cover, and bring to a boil over high heat. Uncover, allow the water to come back to a full, rolling boil, and add the penne and stir. Cook according to the package directions, stirring occasionally. Drain into a large colander and shake the colander to remove excess water from inside the penne. Pour the cooked pasta back into the empty pot. Immediately stir in the oil, peas, and prosciutto. The heat of the pasta will warm the peas and release the flavor of the prosciutto.

3. Serve warm in individual plates or bowls, topped with the Locatelli and pepper.

BISTECCA ALLA FIORENTINA

MAKES 8 SERVINGS

When Mike was growing up in New Jersey, his family ate T-bone steaks with lemon juice at least once a week. Although they were far from rich, there was always plenty of meat on the table. His father, Anthony, manned the grill in season, and in colder weather, steaks were cooked under the broiler. Their version was seasoned with dried oregano, but there is something magical about the scent of fresh rosemary sprigs on a dinner plate.

2 porterhouse steaks, 3 to 3½ pounds each (see Tip)

Salt and ground black pepper

¼ cup extra virgin olive oil

Juice of 3 lemons

8 small sprigs fresh rosemary

1. Preheat the grill to high (glowing embers if using charcoal).

2. Season both sides of the steaks with salt and pepper. Grill for 8 to 10 minutes on the first side, turn, and cook for another 8 to 10 minutes. Check for doneness: for medium-rare, a meat thermometer inserted in the center will read 135°F. Transfer to a large wooden cutting board and let the meat rest for 10 minutes before serving.

3. Cut both sides of the porterhouse—the fillet and the sirloin—away from the bone, and then cut into ¼-inch-thick slices with a very sharp knife.

4. To serve, place one portion of steak on each plate (making sure each guest gets a fair share of sirloin and fillet). Stir together the oil and lemon juice, and drizzle a small amount over each serving. Top each with a sprig of rosemary.

WINE:

*Carpineto Chianti
Classico Riserva*

SANGIOVESE; CHIANTI,
TUSCANY, ITALY

Maintaining a nice equilibrium
between raspberry and vanilla,
this full-bodied Chianti rewards
you with a velvety finish.

OR

*Feudi di San Gregorio
Taurasi DOCG*

AGLIANICO; TAURASI,
CAMPANIA, ITALY

Rich flavors of cherry, red
raspberry, licorice, and baking
spices are a great match for
grilled steak.

TIP: When shopping for porterhouse steaks, make sure you have a good balance of fillet and sirloin. The sirloin will be the longer, larger portion on one side of the bone, and the fillet is the shorter, rounder piece on the other side. Don't be embarrassed to ask the butcher to show you a few steaks in order to choose the best ones possible.

SHAVED FENNEL SALAD

MAKES 8 SERVINGS

Fennel—also known as anise, or *finocchio* in Italy—is eaten before or after a heavy meal for its digestive properties. This light salad is a perfect balance to all the pasta and meat in this dinner.

3 medium or 4 small bulbs fennel

¼ cup olive oil

I orange, zested and juiced

½ teaspoon aniseed

¼ teaspoon salt

Coarsely ground black pepper

WINE:
*Poggio alle Gazze
Toscana IGT Bianco*

SAUVIGNON BLANC;
TUSCANY, ITALY

From Tenuta dell'Ornellaia, a restrained Sauvignon Blanc with vibrant flavors of peach, tropical fruits, and honeysuckle.

1. Cut off the stalks and fronds from the fennel bulbs. Discard the stalks but save the feathery fronds for garnish. Trim and discard the tough bottom ends of the bulbs. Depending on size, cut lengthwise into halves or quarters, and then thinly slice using a mandoline or vegetable slicer. (If you don't have one of these, you can also cut lengthwise along the ribs into thin strips, using a sharp knife.)

2. Place the sliced fennel in a glass bowl. Add the oil, orange juice, aniseed, and salt. Stir until the fennel is evenly dressed.

3. To serve, divide among 8 small plates. Top each serving with a pinch of black pepper and a small amount of orange zest. Garnish with a few feathery fronds.

CINNAMON CARAMELIZED GNOCCHI

MAKES 8 SERVINGS

DeSimone family lore has it that Mike's great-grandmother, Vita Gennaro DeSimone, served this, or some version of it, at Christmas dinner during the Depression. Some accounts of the story have her using ravioli or tortellini, but ricotta was probably a bit of a stretch in a year that almost didn't have dessert.

2 packages (1 pound each) fresh potato or semolina gnocchi

½ pound (2 sticks) butter

½ cup packed brown sugar

½ cup granulated sugar

2 teaspoons ground cinnamon

3 ounces white chocolate, coarsely grated

WINE:
Rosa Regale

SPARKLING DOLCE ROSSO; ACQUI, ITALY

Made from 100 percent Brachetto grapes, this sweet sparkling red tastes of berries tossed with rose petals and almond flowers.

1. Fill a large, heavy-bottomed pot half to two-thirds with water, cover, and bring to a boil over high heat. Stir in the gnocchi and cook according to package directions. Gnocchi float when they are cooked through; be at the ready with a slotted spoon and remove the gnocchi to a plate a few at a time as they float to the surface of the water.

2. Melt the butter in a large, high-sided skillet over medium-high heat. Reduce the heat to medium and add the sugars, stirring constantly. When the sugars are melted, stir in the cinnamon. Add the gnocchi, stirring with a wooden spoon until well coated with the caramelized butter and sugar mix.

3. To serve, divide the hot gnocchi among 8 medium soup or pasta bowls. Top each with a small amount of white chocolate, simulating grated cheese.

13

HEIGHT OF
THE EMPIRE

This meal is a bit more labor-intensive and the dishes tend to be heavier than the other recipes in this cookbook, but let's face it: if you are at the beach and it rains, nothing is more fun than spending the day preparing a sumptuous feast for your family and friends. The flavors are straight out of the Austro-Hungarian Empire, and although deep down this is really simple fare, since you have time on your hands, why not pull out an ornate tablecloth, polish the silver, and fill your biggest vases with flowers from the garden? Sure, nobody wants even one day at the beach to be spoiled by bad weather, but think how happy your guests will be the next time a storm blows in.

APERITIF:
S.A. Prüm Essence Riesling

RIESLING; MOSEL, GERMANY

From the banks of the Mosel River, this lightly sweet white has the flavors of fresh summer apricots and peaches.

APERITIF: *S.A. Prüm Essence Riesling*

PANFRIED QUAIL WITH KIELBASA-STUDDED ORZO
WINE: *Saints Hills Nevina*

VIENNESE STUFFED PEPPERS
WINE: *Matošević Grimalda Red*

CHICKEN PAPRIKASH WITH HOMEMADE BUTTER DUMPLINGS
WINE: *Saints Hills Dingač, St. Lucia Vineyard*

FLAMING APRICOT PALACSINTA
WINE: *Dobogo Mylitta*
DIGESTIVE: *Zwack Liqueur*

PANFRIED QUAIL WITH KIELBASA-STUDDED ORZO

MAKES 8 SERVINGS

Small game birds are present on almost every menu in the Hungarian, Croatian, and Italian countryside. Although many dishes are richly sauced, this simple but elegant preparation is a nice contrast to the rich Chicken Paprikash that follows.

2 tablespoons olive oil

4 tablespoons butter

8 butterflied quail (smile nicely at the butcher and ask her to remove the backbones for you; see Tip)

½ cup white wine

Salt and ground black pepper

Kielbasa-Studded Orzo (recipe follows)

Chopped parsley, for garnish

WINE:
Saints Hills Nevina

MALVASIA ISTRIANA
AND CHARDONNAY;
ISTRIA, CROATIA

This velvety white with flavors of peaches, vanilla, and hazelnut is perfect with the buttery richness of orzo and quail.

1. Heat the oil in a large skillet over medium-high heat. When it's nice and hot, add the butter to melt. Add the quail skin side down and cook until lightly browned, about 5 minutes. Turn over and cook about 3 minutes. Add the wine, reduce the heat to low, cover, and cook for 5 minutes. Add salt and pepper to taste.

2. To serve, place a large spoonful of the orzo in the center of each plate. Arrange a quail in the center of the plate. Garnish with parsley.

TIP: Semi-boned quail are available in many markets. If you are lucky enough to find these, don't worry about asking the butcher to debone them. Cook them breast side down to start.

KIELBASA-STUDDED ORZO

MAKES 8 SERVINGS

This accompaniment to the Panfried Quail requires few ingredients and is easy to make. The orzo is boiled and then fried with onions and kielbasa, a sausage popular in both Polish and Hungarian cuisine. Our Eastern European friends—and you know who you are—can't get enough of this dish.

1 pound orzo

6 tablespoons butter

2 medium onions, finely diced

½ teaspoon salt

½ teaspoon ground black pepper

½ pound kielbasa, finely diced

1. Cook the orzo in 6 quarts of boiling water until al dente, 9 to 11 minutes. Drain in a fine strainer, rinse with cold water, and set aside.

2. Melt 4 tablespoons of the butter in a large skillet over medium-high heat. Add the onions, salt, and pepper and cook until the onions are golden brown. Reduce the heat to medium, add the remaining 2 tablespoons butter, melt, then add the kielbasa and cook about 5 minutes, stirring to prevent sticking.

3. Add the orzo, toss together, cover, and remove from the heat. Set aside until the Panfried Quail is finished and the plates are ready for assembly.

VIENNESE STUFFED PEPPERS

MAKES 8 SERVINGS

Jeff grew up eating stuffed peppers at every holiday dinner. This dish is based on a combination of his grandmother's, his mom's, and his aunt Barbara's recipes.

8 green bell peppers

3 tablespoons butter

2 medium yellow onions, chopped

1½ pounds ground veal

½ pound ground pork

2 cups long-grain rice

1 can (28 ounces) chopped tomatoes

½ teaspoon salt

½ teaspoon ground black pepper

About 4 cups chicken stock

¼ cup chopped parsley, for garnish

WINE:
Matošević Grimalda Red

MERLOT AND TERAN;
ISTRIA, CROATIA

This potent red brimming with the essence of wild berries and earthy spice comes from the Adriatic coast.

1. Cut the tops off the peppers and discard the seeds. Wash and let drain upside down on paper towels.

2. Melt the butter in a large skillet over medium-high heat. Add the onions and cook until golden brown. Push the onions to the perimeter of the pan, add the veal and pork, and cook until lightly browned. Add the rice, tomatoes, salt, and pepper. Combine well and cook for 5 minutes. Remove from the heat.

3. Use a fork to pierce each pepper 2 or 3 times. Spoon the meat-rice mixture into the peppers and stand them upright in a large, heavy-bottomed pot. The peppers should fit somewhat tightly so that they can't fall over. Pour enough stock into the pot to come up to the tops of the peppers, but not over them. Cover with a tight-fitting lid and simmer until the rice is tender, about 40 minutes. Check every 10 minutes and add more stock if necessary (especially if your lid is not so tight). If the rice at the top of the peppers is not cooking, gently stir the rice mixture in each pepper with a teaspoon. Remove from the heat and let rest.

4. To serve, stand and center each pepper on a small plate, and ladle a bit of the sauce on top. Garnish with a sprinkle of chopped parsley.

CHICKEN PAPRIKASH WITH HOMEMADE BUTTER DUMPLINGS

MAKES 8 SERVINGS

This is well suited to those cool late-summer evenings. It requires little advance preparation but basically takes about 45 minutes start to finish. Jeff's mother taught him not to be afraid of full-fat sour cream; it will give you the proper consistency, it tastes better, and, most important, sweater weather is right around the corner.

8 tablespoons (1 stick) butter

4 medium onions, cut into medium dice

16 skin-on, bone-in chicken thighs

1 teaspoon salt

2 teaspoons ground black pepper

5 tablespoons good-quality Hungarian paprika

About 4 cups chicken stock

3 tablespoons all-purpose flour

16 ounces full-fat sour cream, plus ¼ cup for garnish

Homemade Butter Dumplings (recipe follows)

1. Melt 4 tablespoons of the butter in a large skillet over medium-high heat. Add the onions and cook until translucent but slightly golden. Remove the onions from the pan and set aside. Melt the remaining 4 tablespoons butter in the pan and add the chicken thighs, skin side down. Season with the salt, pepper, and 4 tablespoons of the paprika. Cook until browned, about 7 minutes. Turn over to cook the other side until lightly browned, about 5 minutes. Add enough chicken stock to partially cover the chicken. Return the fried onions to the pan, cover, and simmer for 35 minutes. Stir frequently.

2. Mix together the flour and remaining 1 tablespoon paprika in a small bowl or measuring cup. Whisk in the 16 ounces sour cream in small increments, making sure to combine well.

3. Remove the chicken from the skillet and set aside while you finish the paprika sauce. Stir a few tablespoons of liquid from the pan into the sour cream mixture and whisk. Continue, adding a few tablespoons at a time, whisking constantly, until the pan is essentially empty. This will prevent lumps from forming and give you a silky-smooth paprika sauce. Return the chicken to the pan and cover completely with the paprika sauce. Simmer for about 5 minutes to heat through.

4. To serve, scoop a few of the homemade dumplings into the center of each dinner plate. Place 2 thighs on each plate and ladle over them a sufficient amount of paprika sauce to form a nice puddle. Garnish with a spoonful of sour cream. Enjoy! (And promise yourself you'll do extra cardio at the gym tomorrow.)

HOMEMADE BUTTER DUMPLINGS

MAKES 8 SERVINGS

These dumplings are easy to make and take only a few minutes. The longest part of the recipe is waiting for the chicken stock to boil. If you don't have enough time or are feeling lazy, you can easily boil some store-bought wide egg noodles to go with the Chicken Paprikash.

2¼ cups sifted all-purpose flour

2 teaspoons baking powder

¾ teaspoon salt

8 tablespoons (1 stick) butter, at room temperature

½ cup plus 2 tablespoons whole milk

8 cups chicken stock

1. Combine the flour, baking powder, and salt in a bowl. Add the butter a little at a time, and mix with your hands until you have the consistency of small "pebbles." Add the milk and continue mixing the dough with your hands until smooth yet stiff.

2. Bring the chicken stock to a boil in a saucepan.

3. Meanwhile, roll the dough out on a floured cutting board to about ⅛-inch thickness. Using a sharp knife, cut the dough into 1-inch squares, then diagonally into triangles. We go for the more irregular style—it lets your guests know that your dumplings really are made by hand.

4. Drop the dumplings into the boiling chicken stock one at a time. Boil in 2 to 3 batches, for 8 to 10 minutes each. Remove with a slotted spoon and place on a warm plate until ready to serve.

FLAMING APRICOT PALACSINTA

MAKES 8 SERVINGS

Our Fire Island housemates—especially the single ones—always pretend that they don't want to eat dessert, but when they see the flames shooting out of the kitchen, they loosen their belts a notch, sit back, and dig into these delicious apricot-filled *palacsinta*.

6 tablespoons butter, plus extra for cooking the *palacsinta*

2½ cups all-purpose flour

4 teaspoons sugar

¼ teaspoon salt

5 eggs

2½ cups whole milk

12 ounces apricot jam

3 ounces apricot brandy (see Tip)

WINE:
Dobogo Mylitta
FURMINT; TOKAJ, HUNGARY

This ethereal sweet dessert wine with notes of caramelized stone fruits combines beautifully with the rich dessert.

1. Melt 2 tablespoons of the butter in the microwave. Combine the flour, sugar, and salt in a bowl. Using a hand mixer, beat the eggs and milk in a large glass bowl. Slowly beat in the dry ingredients until you have a smooth runny batter. Add the melted butter and mix for an additional 10 seconds. Let the batter rest in the refrigerator for 20 minutes. Mix again just before use.

2. Heat an 8-inch crêpe pan (or an omelet pan) and melt 1 teaspoon butter. Ladle ¼ cup batter into the pan and roll the pan around so the bottom is coated evenly. When the edges of the *palacsinta* turn golden brown, flip and cook the other side for about 30 seconds. Stack the finished *palacsinta* on a warm plate and set aside.

3. Spread 2 teaspoons of apricot jam on each *palacsinta*, fold into quarters, and refrigerate. These can be made earlier in the day or even a few days before.

(continued)

DIGESTIVE:
Zwack Liqueur

BUDAPEST, HUNGARY

A mysterious blend of over forty herbs and spices, Zwack (called Unicum in Hungary) was developed by the Hapsburg court physician over two hundred years ago. Now the national drink of Hungary, it is a delicious and practically medicinal nightcap.

4. When you're ready to serve the dessert, melt 4 tablespoons butter in a large skillet. Add the folded *palacsinta* and cook until they are warmed thoroughly and starting to turn golden brown. Carefully add the apricot brandy and ignite with a long wooden match. Your guests will surely be impressed—but be careful to stand back so you don't singe your eyebrows off. (Yes, we know this from experience!) After the flames have died down, place 2 *palacsinta* on each plate and serve.

TIP: If you don't have apricot brandy, almost any liquor over 80 proof you have kicking around the house will do. Just don't use grain alcohol or 151-proof rum—the results could be disastrous.

14

LABOR DAY CARIBBEAN BARBECUE

Ahh, Labor Day! Just because the calendar says summer is officially over doesn't mean we can't drag our beachgoing days out a little longer. September is one of the most beautiful times of the year on Fire Island or in any seaside town—and it's also the month that we start planning our warm-weather winter getaways. One of our favorite places to head when the mercury drops is the Grace Bay Club in Turks and Caicos, which is where we picked up some of the ideas and flavors for this menu. With a superb balance of sweet and spicy notes, the food of the Caribbean lends itself well to hot summer days with a touch of coolness at night. Except for dessert, this menu is designed to be served all at once; it's a barbecue, so relax and have fun!

Open a bottle of rum, ice down a tub filled with wine bottles, add a little reggae and steel drum to your playlist, and soon you'll be dancing around the pool with a plate of ribs in your hand and scheduling a winter beach holiday with your family and friends.

MIKE'S CARIBBEAN SPICED RIBS

BBQ JERK CHICKEN

MANGO AND BLACK BEAN SALSA

RED BEANS AND RICE

SAUTÉED PIÑA COLADA

Wine is not made in the Caribbean, but there are plenty of wines that pair well with the hot and sweet notes of tropical cuisine. We recommend choosing a few whites and reds from the New World and the Southern Hemisphere and letting your guests serve themselves. Make sure to have a few bottles of rum on hand as well. We served this exact menu to our friends in our New York City backyard recently, and Craggy Range winemaker Steve Smith was one of the invited guests. He showed up with two cases of his wonderful reds and whites from New Zealand, and our "End of Summer Rum Party" quickly turned into a Craggy Range Party. We are still trying to finish off all of the leftover rum!

WHITE WINE:

Thelema Sauvignon Blanc

SAUVIGNON BLANC; STELLENBOSCH, SOUTH AFRICA

Intense flavors of grapefruit and lime are punctuated by pleasing herbal notes.

Craggy Range Te Muna Road Vineyard Sauvignon Blanc

SAUVIGNON BLANC; MARTINBOROUGH, NEW ZEALAND

Steve Smith's outstanding wine is redolent of apple, white peach, and mango.

De Martino Legado Reserva Chardonnay

CHARDONNAY; LIMARÍ VALLEY, CHILE

Aging in oak barrels adds buttery richness to flavors of tropical fruits.

Nobilo Icon Sauvignon Blanc

SAUVIGNON BLANC; MARLBOROUGH, NEW ZEALAND

Clean minerality shines through notes of orange rind and grapefruit.

Frankland Estate Isolation Ridge Riesling

RIESLING; FRANKLAND RIVER, WESTERN AUSTRALIA

Green apple and light citrus scents are imbued with a white floral undercurrent.

RED WINE:

Bellingham Dragon's Lair

SHIRAZ BLEND; FRANSCHHOEK, SOUTH AFRICA

Blackberry, red cherry, smoke, and clove notes are well suited to sweet and spicy Caribbean food.

Neil Ashmead GTS Grand Tourer Shiraz

SHIRAZ; BAROSSA, AUSTRALIA

Shiraz has long been the go-to wine for barbecued meats, and this jammy Aussie won't disappoint.

De Toren Z

MERLOT–CABERNET SAUVIGNON BLEND; STELLENBOSCH, SOUTH AFRICA

Intense berry flavors with scents of baking spices and leather make this Bordeaux-style blend the sophisticated choice for dining under the stars.

Kim Crawford Pinot Noir

PINOT NOIR; MARLBOROUGH, NEW ZEALAND

A strawberry and cherry opening is joined by subtle vanilla notes picked up in the barrel.

Rutherglen Estates Mr. Chairman

MOURVEDRE-SHIRAZ BLEND; RUTHERGLEN, VICTORIA, AUSTRALIA

Penetrating qualities of cherry and wood are followed by gentler touches of violet and spice.

RUM FOR MIXING:

Mount Gay Eclipse Silver

BARBADOS, WEST INDIES

Clean and pure, an excellent rum to blend with a variety of mixers.

Bacardi Ron 8 Años

PUERTO RICO

Aged eight years, one of the Bacardi family's premium products.

RUM FOR SIPPING:

Patron Spirits Pyrat XO Reserve Rum

GUYANA

Rich caramel notes with nuance of butterscotch.

Mount Gay 1703 Cask Selection

BARBADOS, WEST INDIES

Elegant spice, caramel, and leather notes combined with robust flavor are the reasons to enjoy this rum in a snifter.

MIKE'S CARIBBEAN SPICED RIBS

MAKES 8 SERVINGS

We took several Caribbean trips in order to do our due diligence to the rum trade. On each we picked up bottles of rum from duty-free that are not readily available in the States, and we also purchased some extras to serve at our end-of-the-summer party. Although we fed our guests plenty of appetizers, we could not keep these ribs on the platter as they came sizzling off the grill—our friends were standing around waiting to grab the red-hot pork off Mike's tongs. They are steamed first and then finished on the grill, which accounts for their moist interior and crispy exterior.

I pound brown sugar

I ½ tablespoons salt

2 teaspoons dried sage

2 teaspoons cayenne pepper

I teaspoon ground cumin

I teaspoon curry powder

24 baby back pork ribs

1. Mix together the brown sugar, salt, and spices in a glass bowl. Arrange the ribs in a large glass baking dish or platter, sprinkle the brown sugar and spice mix over the meat, and turn by hand and "pack" the sugar mixture on to coat completely. Refrigerate for 2 to 4 hours.

2. Preheat the oven to 350°F. Using a broiler pan with a slotted rack, remove the rack and add about ½ inch water to the bottom of the pan. Replace the slotted rack and arrange the ribs on the rack. (The water will be below the ribs—they will be sitting on the top of the pan, *not* in the water.) Repack any brown sugar mixture left in the glass pan around the ribs and roast for 30 minutes. Remove from the oven and let cool on the broiler pan. (Remember to hold the pan level while placing in and removing from the oven, so you don't spill the water.) The ribs can be steamed early in the day, or even a day or two in advance. If preparing the same day, store on a plate in the refrigerator, or if in advance, refrigerate in an airtight container. If refrigerated, let sit at room temperature for 30 minutes prior to grilling.

3. Preheat the grill to high. Place the ribs one at a time on the grill with tongs. When all the ribs are on the grill, count to 30, then begin turning the ribs, one at a time, starting with the first one on the grill and going in order. After all your ribs are turned, count to 30 again, and start transferring them to a clean platter.

BBQ JERK CHICKEN

MAKES 8 SERVINGS

After a morning of scuba diving in the pristine waters off Turks and Caicos, we asked some locals where they go for jerk chicken. The answer was almost always the same: "We don't go out for jerk—we make it at home." When pressed, they all came up with the same roadside jerk stand. The chicken we ate there was moist and delicious, with just the right symmetry of sweetness and spice. It took us a while to come up with a good recipe, but now you don't have to go out for jerk, either; you can make it at home. The heat in traditional "jerk" is usually provided by Scotch bonnet peppers, which are not so easy to locate. You can replace the red pepper flakes and cayenne with two small dried crumbled Scotch bonnets if you can find them.

2 cups packed dark brown sugar

1 cup honey

½ cup white rum

6 tablespoons distilled white vinegar

½ cup dried onion flakes

¼ cup dried thyme

2 tablespoons ground allspice

4 teaspoons red pepper flakes

2 teaspoons salt

1 teaspoon cayenne pepper

16 bone-in, skin-on chicken thighs

1. Combine everything but the chicken in a large glass bowl. Reserve ½ cup of the marinade to use as a baste. Add the chicken to the marinade a few pieces at a time, turning until coated. Transfer to 1-gallon resealable plastic bags or covered plastic containers. Divide any remaining marinade evenly among the bags or containers of chicken, and place in the refrigerator to marinate for at least 4 hours. (This can even be done 2 days in advance.)

2. Preheat the oven to 350°F. Lightly oil a rimmed baking sheet. Arrange the chicken skin side up on the baking sheet and roast for 35 minutes. The chicken will be finished on the grill; it can be roasted up to a few hours in advance, or grilled right after it comes out of the oven.

3. Preheat the grill to high (or glowing embers if using charcoal). Place the chicken skin side up on the grill grate. Using a long-handled barbecue brush, brush the top of the chicken with the reserved baste. Grill for 2 minutes, turn, and grill skin side down for 2 minutes. Carefully remove the chicken from the grill with tongs (the chicken skin may stick to the grate) and serve hot.

MANGO AND BLACK BEAN SALSA

MAKES 8 SERVINGS

Trying to sail to India for spices, Christopher Columbus instead found his way to an island in the Caribbean, and accidentally discovered "America." It took several hundred years for the people, spices, and fruits of India to make their way to the turquoise waters off the Americas, but mangoes are now as much a part of the cuisine of the Caribbean as of their native India.

2 to 3 large mangoes, ripe but still firm to the touch

2 cans (15 ounces each) small black beans, drained and rinsed

1 large red onion, finely diced

Juice of 2 limes

1 jalapeño pepper, seeded and finely diced (see Tip)

1. Score the skin of each mango lengthwise into quarters, then peel back and remove the skin. Cut as much mango as you can away from the pit and cut into small cubes. If the mango is overripe, you may end up with a lot of shapeless pulp—but that is fine; it is all usable.

2. Combine the mango, beans, onion, lime juice, and jalapeño in a glass or ceramic bowl, cover with plastic wrap, and refrigerate until ready to serve.

TIP: When cutting jalapeños, it is a good idea to wear rubber kitchen gloves, or even disposable latex gloves. This makes the slicing a little more difficult, but you will avoid getting capsaicin—the substance that gives peppers their heat—into your eyes or mouth. If you don't have rubber gloves in your house, wash your hands thoroughly with soap and water and dry them well immediately after handling the jalapeño.

RED BEANS AND RICE

MAKES 8 SERVINGS

Rice and beans is a staple throughout the Caribbean, on both the islands and the mainland of Central and South America. At the end of the season, as the cooler weather sets in and next summer seems too far away to contemplate, this dish—and in fact this whole meal—can start you thinking about where to plan your warm-weather winter getaway.

3 tablespoons olive oil

2 tablespoons butter

2 small red onions, cut into medium dice

4 cups chicken stock

I pound long-grain rice

2 cans (15 ounces each) small red beans, drained and rinsed

½ cup frozen peas, thawed

I red bell pepper, finely diced

I teaspoon red pepper flakes

Salt and ground black pepper

1. Heat the oil in a medium saucepan over medium-high heat, and then add the butter. When the butter is melted, add the onions, reduce the heat to medium, and stir until wilted, about 3 minutes. Stir in the chicken stock and rice, cover, and bring to a boil over high heat, occasionally stirring the rice. Reduce the heat to medium and cook, covered, for 10 to 15 minutes.

2. Stir in the beans, peas, bell pepper, red pepper flakes, and salt and black pepper to taste. Cook over low to medium heat, uncovered, stirring frequently, until the rice is tender, about 10 minutes. If all the stock is absorbed but the rice is still not tender, stir in small amounts of water or chicken stock to keep the rice soft and pliable, salting to taste if adding water. Set aside, covered. (If made in advance, reheat over low heat, stirring frequently, and adding small amounts of liquid if necessary.)

SAUTÉED PIÑA COLADA

MAKES 8 SERVINGS

For many people, a piña colada is the ultimate tropical drink. This fun confection is a twist on the typical umbrella-topped combo of rum, pineapple, and coconut, and it is a fantastic finish to your meal and your summer.

3 pineapples

8 ounces white rum

8 tablespoons (I stick) butter

½ cup packed light brown sugar

½ cup flaked coconut

1. Peel, core, and quarter the pineapples. Halve each quarter lengthwise for a total of 24 "spears." Arrange the pineapple spears in a large glass baking dish, overlapping as necessary, and pour the rum over the pineapple. Cover the dish with plastic wrap and set aside for several hours.

2. Heat a large skillet over medium heat. Add the butter and melt, stirring with a wooden spoon. Add the brown sugar and continue to stir until the sugar melts and begins to bubble. Using tongs, add the pineapple slices a few at a time, and cook for 2 to 3 minutes, turning once. Transfer the pineapple to a small platter and repeat until all the pineapple is cooked. (It is a good idea to have extra butter and brown sugar on hand, and add small amounts as necessary between batches.)

3. To serve, arrange 3 spears of sautéed pineapple per guest on a small plate and drizzle with a teaspoon of the rum marinade (see Tip). Sprinkle a little coconut over the pineapple. If you would never drink a piña colada without a paper umbrella, who are we to stop you from decorating your dessert with one?

TIP: Reserve the remaining pineapple-infused rum to make poolside drinks tomorrow afternoon, because, after all, "Tomorrow is another day!"

ACKNOWLEDGMENTS

We would like to thank the following people, without whom *The Fire Island Cookbook* would not have been possible. We are very grateful to our amazing editor, Emily Bestler, who first got to know us through our recipes and has made this journey an absolute pleasure. We have also enjoyed working with the lovely Kate Cetrulo, the ever-smiling Caroline Porter, and the wonderful team at Emily Bestler Books, Atria, and Simon & Schuster. A million thanks to our indefatigable manager, Peter Miller, and his wonderful assistant, Adrienne Rosado. Heartfelt thanks to our talented photographer, Frances Janisch, and to our brilliant stylist Paul Lowe and his assistant, Michaela Hayes. We would also like to thank our mothers, Paula DeSimone and Marge Jenssen, who gave us each our start in the kitchen. No expression of gratitude would be complete without mentioning the friends with whom we have shared many wonderful meals, especially Jim, Randy, Jim, Mark, Stephen, Julie, Tammy, Denise, Vincent, Sue, Cris, Ian, Lucy, Latice, Chris, Robin, Ana Paula, Marcelo, Carmen, Alexandra, Mavi, and Vicente. Many thanks to all of you for being a part of our lives, our meals, and this book.

INDEX